MYSTERIES, LEGENDS, AND UNEXPLAINED PHENOMENA

WITCHES AND WICCANS

MYSTERIES, LEGENDS, AND UNEXPLAINED PHENOMENA

MYSTERIES, LEGENDS, AND UNEXPLAINED PHENOMENA

WITCHES AND WICCANS

ROSEMARY ELLEN GUILEY

CHELSEA HOUSE
PUBLISHERS
An imprint of Infobase Publishing

WITCHES AND WICCANS

Chelsea House
An imprint of Infobase Publishing
132 West 31st Street
New York NY 10001

Library of Congress Cataloging-in-Publication Data
Guiley, Rosemary.
 Witches and Wiccans / Rosemary Ellen Guiley.
   p. cm. — (Mysteries, legends, and unexplained phenomena)
 Includes bibliographical references and index.
 ISBN-13: 978-0-7910-9397-9
 ISBN-10: 0-7910-9397-2
 1. Witchcraft. 2. Wicca. I. Title. II. Series.

 BF1566.G855 2008
 133.4'3—dc22

                    2008022658

Text design by James Scotto-Lavino
Cover design by Ben Peterson

Printed in the United States of America   **3 1561 00228 9563**

Bang EJB 10 9 8 7 6 5 4 3 2 1

This book is printed on acid-free paper.

Contents

Foreword

Did you ever have an experience that turned your whole world upside down? Maybe you saw a ghost or a UFO. Perhaps you had an unusual, vivid dream that seemed real. Maybe you suddenly knew that a certain event was going to happen in the future. Or, perhaps you saw a creature or a being that did not fit the description of anything known in the natural world. At first you might have thought your imagination was playing tricks on you. Then, perhaps, you wondered about what you experienced and went looking for an explanation.

Every day and night people have experiences they can't explain. For many people these events are life changing. Their comfort zone of what they can accept as "real" is put to the test. It takes only one such experience for people to question the reality of the mysterious worlds that might exist beyond the one we live in. Perhaps you haven't encountered the unknown, but you have an intense curiosity about it. Either way, by picking up this book, you've started an adventure to explore and learn more, and you've come to the right place! The book you hold has been written by a leading expert in the paranormal–someone who understands unusual experiences and who knows the answers to your questions.

As a seeker of knowledge, you have plenty of company. Mythology, folklore, and records of the past show that human beings have had paranormal experiences throughout history. Even prehistoric cave paintings and gravesites indicate that early humans had concepts of the supernatural and of an afterlife. Humans have always sought to understand paranormal experiences and to put them into a frame of reference that makes sense to us in our daily lives. Some of the greatest minds in history have grappled with questions about the paranormal. For example, Greek philosopher Plato pondered the nature of dreams and how we "travel" during them. Isaac Newton was interested in the esoteric study of alchemy, which has magical elements, and St. Thomas Aquinas explored the nature of angels and spirits. Philosopher William James joined organizations dedicated to psychical research; and even the inventor of the light bulb, Thomas Alva Edison, wanted to build a device that could talk to the dead. More recently, physicists such as David Bohm, Stephen Hawking, William Tiller, and Michio Kaku have developed ideas that may help explain how and why paranormal phenomena happen, and neuroscience researchers like Michael Persinger have explored the nature of consciousness.

Exactly what is a paranormal experience or phenomenon? "Para" is derived from a Latin term for "beyond." So "paranormal" means "beyond normal," or things that do not fit what we experience through our five senses alone and which do not follow the laws we observe in nature and in science. Paranormal experiences and phenomena run the gamut from the awesome and marvelous, such as angels and miracles, to the downright terrifying, such as vampires and werewolves.

Paranormal experiences have been consistent throughout the ages, but explanations of them have changed as societies, cultures, and technologies have changed. For example, our ancestors were much closer to the invisible realms. In times when life was simpler, they saw, felt, and experienced other realities on a daily basis. When night fell, the darkness was thick and quiet, and it was easier to see unusual things, such as ghosts. They had no electricity to keep the night lit up. They had no media for constant communication and entertainment. Travel was difficult. They had more time to notice subtle things that were just beyond their ordinary senses. Few doubted their experiences. They accepted the invisible realms as an extension of ordinary life.

Today, we have many distractions. We are constantly busy, from the time we wake up until we go to bed. The world is full of light and noise 24 hours a day, seven days a week. We have television, the Internet, computer games, and cell phones to keep us busy, busy, busy.

We are ruled by technology and science. Yet, we still have paranormal experiences very similar to those of our ancestors. Because these occurrences do not fit neatly into science and technology, many people think they are illusions, and there are plenty of skeptics always ready to debunk the paranormal and reinforce that idea.

In roughly the past 100 years, though, some scientists have studied the paranormal and attempted to find scientific evidence for it. Psychic phenomena have proven difficult to observe and measure according to scientific standards. However, lack of scientific proof does not mean paranormal experiences do not happen. Courageous scientists are still looking for bridges between science and the supernatural.

My personal experiences are behind my lifelong study of the paranormal. Like many children I had invisible playmates when I was very young, and I saw strange lights in the yard and woods that I instinctively knew were the nature spirits who lived there. Children seem to be very open to paranormal phenomena, but their ability to have these experiences often fades away as they become more involved in the outside world, or, perhaps, as adults tell them not to believe in what they experience, that it's only in their imagination. Even when I was very young, I was puzzled that other people would tell me with great authority that I did not experience what I knew I did.

A major reason for my interest in the paranormal is precognitive dreaming experienced by members of my family. Precognition means "fore knowing," or knowing the future. My mother had a lot of psychic experiences, including dreams of future events. As a teen it seemed amazing to me that dreams could show us the future. I was determined to learn more about this and to have such dreams myself. I found books that explained extrasensory perception, the knowing of information beyond the five senses. I learned about dreams and experimented with them. I taught myself to visit distant places in my dreams and to notice details about them that I could later verify in the physical world. I learned how to send people telepathic messages in dreams and how to receive messages in dreams. Every night became an exciting adventure.

Those interests led me to other areas of the paranormal. Pretty soon I was engrossed in studying all kinds of topics. I learned different techniques for divination, including the Tarot. I learned how to meditate. I took courses to develop my own psychic skills, and I gave psychic readings to others. Everyone has at least some natural psychic ability and can improve it with attention and practice.

Next I turned my attention to the skies, to ufology, and what might be "out there" in space. I studied the lore of angels and fairies. I delved into the dark shadowy realm of demons and monsters. I learned the principles of real magic and spell-casting. I undertook investigations of haunted places. I learned how to see auras and do energy healing. I even participated in some formal scientific laboratory experiments for telepathy.

My studies led me to have many kinds of experiences that have enriched my understanding of the paranormal. I cannot say that I can prove anything in scientific terms. It may be some time yet before science and the paranormal stop flirting with each other and really get together. Meanwhile, we can still learn a great deal from our personal experiences. At the very least, our paranormal experiences contribute to our inner wisdom. I encourage others to do the same as I do. Look first for natural explanations of strange phenomena. If natural explanations cannot be found or seem unlikely, consider paranormal explanations. Many paranormal experiences fall into a vague area, where although natural causes might exist, we simply don't know what could explain them. In that case I tell people to trust their intuition that they had a paranormal experience. Sometimes the explanation makes itself known later on.

I have concluded from my studies and experiences that invisible dimensions are layered upon our world, and that many paranormal experiences occur when there are openings between worlds. The doorways often open at unexpected times. You take a trip, visit a haunted place, or have a strange dream—and suddenly reality shifts. You get a glimpse behind the curtain that separates the ordinary from the extraordinary.

The books in this series will introduce you to these exciting and mysterious subjects. You'll learn many things that will astonish you. You'll be given lots of tips for how to explore the paranormal on your own. Paranormal investigation is a popular field, and you don't have to be a scientist or a full-time researcher to explore it. There are many things you can do in your free time. The knowledge you gain from these books will help prepare you for any unusual and unexpected experiences.

As you go deeper into your study of the paranormal, you may come up with new ideas for explanations. That's one of the appealing aspects of paranormal investigation—there is always room for bold ideas. So, keep an open and curious mind, and think big. Mysterious worlds are waiting for you!

—Rosemary Ellen Guiley

Introduction

Witchcraft is a powerful word, one that calls up images of dark and secret rituals, wild supernatural forces, and mysterious spirits summoned on command. Thanks to stories, films, and even history, many people may think of witches as ugly, mean people who can turn a person into a toad. They may be right—and they may be wrong! Of all the occult arts, witchcraft is one of the most misunderstood.

Witchcraft is a form of sorcery and involves the magical ability to cast spells. People who possess these supernatural powers have been part of human society since the earliest times. Magic itself is neither good nor bad, but neutral. It is a tool that can be used for positive spells like healing and protection or negative spells like cursing and harming.

There is plenty of evidence that witches have performed good services. Yet around the globe and throughout history, witches have been regarded as dark and dangerous people. Perhaps it is because people feared that the power witches seemed to possess might be easily turned against them rather than used to help them. Don't anger a witch or else!

Witchcraft has had a particularly rough ride in the history of Western civilization. As Christianity spread throughout Europe, witchcraft came to be associated with the Devil. It was considered not just dark and dangerous, but demonic and, according to authorities, part of the Devil's plan to destroy souls. For several centuries during the Inquisition, people accused of witchcraft were tortured and executed in a terrible campaign of terror. The Inquisition began in the twelfth century as part of the Catholic Church's efforts to eliminate rival religious groups. In the late 1400s the church declared witchcraft a crime of heresy. During the next two centuries, there were many trials and executions of accused witches. Protestants also joined the witch hunts. The witch trials declined in the 1700s, and the Inquisition came to an end by the start of the 1800s.

Many of the stereotypes from those days linger in the contemporary world. Broom-riding, cauldron-stirring, cackling hags remain a common depiction of witches in the media and popular culture. To make matters more confusing, there are now many people who practice Witchcraft, or Wicca, as a religion. They say that they are honoring the Divine, especially the divine feminine as the Goddess, as well as the forces of the natural world. They emphasize using magic for good. For them, Witchcraft is a path of spiritual growth, as other religions are for other people.

Burning of accused witches in a German marketplace during the Inquisition.
(Bettmann/Corbis)

In this book, we will sort through the myths, facts, and fallacies about witchcraft and look at the similarities and differences between witchcraft the sorcery and Witchcraft the religion.

Chapter 1, "Boiling Up A Pot of Trouble," provides an overview of witches and their place in society. What were witches like in ancient times, and what are they like today?

Chapter 2, "The Inquisition's Reign of Terror," describes the witch hysteria that swept through Europe and even the North American colonies. People were terrified of witchcraft and religious authorities, and opportunists seized on that fear to further their own agendas. The authorized murders committed by inquisitors raise questions about which side really committed acts of evil.

Chapter 3, "Anatomy of a Witch Trial and Execution," will visit some trials to see how innocent people were often framed as witches.

Chapter 4, "Witchcraft in Early America," looks at witchcraft beliefs and practices that were seeded in colonial times, and how they were adapted to the New World. Particular attention is given to "pow-wowing," a unique blend of folk magic that is part of the Pennsylvania Dutch culture.

America's most famous witch case, the Salem hysteria of 1691-92, is examined in Chapter 5, "Witchcraze in Salem." Amazingly, children playing divination games triggered the hysteria. At the time, high social, religious, and political tensions made Salem a disaster waiting to happen.

Chapter 6, "The Old Religion Comes Out of the Broom Closet," moves into modern times when Witchcraft was "rediscovered" or reinvented as a religion. Some colorful personalities placed witchcraft on the front pages. Witchcraft the religion managed to survive the early sensationalism and take hold as a genuine spiritual path.

"Wicca and the Goddess," Chapter 7, goes further into religious Witchcraft, also called Wicca. Here, we look at such questions as: How did this new religion evolve? Who were the key players? And what attracts people to Witchcraft as a religion?

Chapter 8, "Becoming a Witch/Wiccan," looks at how a person becomes a Witch, the activities of a coven, and how Witches have pursued their religious civil rights.

"Spellcraft," Chapter 9, covers the magical side of Wicca, the tools, magical circles, and types of spells modern Witches use.

Chapter 10, "Wiccan Celebrations," describes the Wheel of the Year, the seasonal festivals that make up the Wiccan calendar of holy days.

In addition, there is a timeline of major historical points, a glossary of key terms, and suggestions for more research.

Enjoy this tour of witchcraft. You will find that common ideas about witchcraft may be wrong. Witchcraft is ever fascinating, deep, and mysterious. It reveals a great deal about the light and the dark sides of human nature.

Boiling Up A Pot of Trouble

In ancient Rome a well-respected married woman has become the target of nasty gossip swirling around a scandal involving her husband. She tried to ignore it, but a few of her jealous enemies keep tearing her down. It's time for action: she will consult the "Egyptian woman," the local witch.

The Egyptian woman is an old hag who lives on the outskirts of town. People are afraid of her, and they leave her alone—unless they need her services. And they need them often. Magic is a common way to remedy problems. No one knows exactly how the Egyptian woman got her powers, but it is said that the talking spirits in the temples of her homeland bestowed them upon her.

The hag listens to her client describe her enemies and how she wants them silenced. The solution: a **binding** spell, which stops someone from doing harm.

Using three fingers, the Egyptian woman places three pieces of incense beneath the threshold of the door. She takes threads and ties them around a piece of dark lead, while she mutters magical **charms** in a low voice. Then she puts seven beans in her mouth and mumbles more charms. She takes a fish, smears its head with pitch, sews its mouth shut, drops wine upon it, and roasts it over the fire in her hearth. She and the client drink the wine that is left over.

"Now," the hag says, "we have bound the hostile tongues and spiteful mouths."

In Alexandria, Egypt, a young woman named Simaetha is worried that she has lost the interest of her lover, a handsome young athlete. They fell in love at first sight, but now she has not seen him for 11 days. If he won't return to her on his own, she will force him to come back with magic.

Simaetha has gone through town, consulting every sorcerer and hag witch she can find, but none of the spells cast by them has worked. In desperation she decides to do magic herself and assembles in her home the ingredients and tools.

On the night of the full moon, she stirs up potions of wine, milk, and water with barley groats, bay leaves, bran, wax, coltsfoot, and pulverized lizard. She is fortunate to have kept a fringe from her lover's cloak, and she shreds it over the fire, uttering spells and incantations to the moon and the fierce goddess of the underworld, Hecate. She raises up supernatural energy with a magical wheel, a bull-roarer, and a bronze gong.

The two cases above are taken from descriptions in classical literature. The bean-chewing hag comes from *Fasti* by Ovid (43 BCE-17 CE), a Roman poet.[1] Simaethea's witchcraft comes from *Pharmakeutriai* ("The Witches") by Theocritus (c. 310-250 BCE), a Greek poet who wrote about everyday life in Alexandria.[2]

Classical poets and writers composed many tales involving sorcerers and witches, describing their rituals in detail. They drew on real situations for their ideas. In the ancient world, witchcraft and magic were part of daily life. People turned to magic for everything from healing minor wounds to luring back straying lovers, and from winning a political competition to gaining the advantage in warfare. Witches and sorcerers were not well regarded, but they were tolerated. They were believed to possess dark and fearsome powers and to command the elements, the stars, and the attention of the gods.

Witches (female) and sorcerers (male) were not the only ones who practiced magical arts. Priests, healers, and miracle-workers, called *thaumaturgists*, performed divine magic as well, and often enjoyed better reputations than witches.

WHAT IS WITCHCRAFT?

Belief in witchcraft is found everywhere, but there is no universal definition of "witchcraft." Witchcraft, sorcery, and magic are three terms that can have very different meanings among people and in different historical time periods. They all involve the use of supernatural power and the intervention of spirits or gods to achieve a purpose. Witchcraft and sorcery are types of magic.

Magic is as old as humanity. It probably began with attempts to control and improve food supplies, survival, and the elements. As civilizations developed, magic became more sophisticated, expanding into controlling the actions, circumstances, and emotions of others, thus changing the future and destiny of peoples and nations.

Magic is a neutral power. It can be good or bad, depending on how it is used. Witchcraft has often been regarded as the low end of magic—spells and **curses** used for dark purposes. Sorcery has a dark reputation, too, though in some cultures it is respected as much as religion. In Western history the witch became, like the Devil, a symbol of extreme evil. A modern religious movement called Witchcraft or Wicca presents witches in a much more positive light.

The word "witch" comes from the Middle English word *witche*, derived from the Old English terms *wicca*, *wicce*, and *wiccian*, which mean "to work sorcery, bewitch."[3] The Indo-European root of these terms is *weik*, which has to do with magic and religion. It is often hard to separate witchcraft from other forms of magic and even from elements of religion.

ROOTS OF WITCHCRAFT

Primitive, early human beings probably accidentally discovered ways to influence the forces of nature and to see the future and the realms of invisible spirits. Certain individuals may have been born with apparent supernatural power and learned by trial and error how to use it. Some form of magic arose in all ancient societies and civilizations. The characteristics of it are similar no matter where and when it existed, and many of those early traditions survived to the present.

Several types of magic evolved early. One involved summoning spirits for help. The people who possessed supernatural power, such as psychic ability, could see spirits and intuitively understand the forces of nature. They discovered that, when in certain states of mind, they could call upon those spirits and forces to ask for certain things

Portrait of a Witch

The familiar Halloween witch is an old hag with a warty face, big nose, pointy chin, and black hat, flying on a broom. Is that what a witch is supposed to look like? Where did this image come from?

Perhaps because witches have been associated with evil for many thousands of years, it is natural to assume they are ugly. Witches can be either female or male, but usually witches are thought to be women.

In Greek mythology, Hecate, an ugly hag goddess, rules magic, witchcraft, the underworld, and the dark side of the moon. Witches were believed to invoke Hecate in their spells and to practice necromancy, summoning the dead from the underworld for fortune-telling. But plenty of witches in classical literature were beautiful and enchanting, not ugly.

Hags appear often in folklore and stories, where they are sometimes benevolent, wise, beautiful, and forever young. In Irish and Scottish lore, good hags help with spinning cloth. Other hags are associated with creeping horrors of the supernatural world and have terrifying appearances themselves.

No one knows exactly where the pointed witch's hat originated. Most likely it is an artist's interpretation, perhaps from the nineteenth century, to happen. Influencing nature was vital to survival, so the magical person who could make it rain, for example, acquired a great deal of importance.

Another type of magic came to be called "sympathetic magic." This means that the magical effect can be transferred from one thing to another. Sympathetic magic is the principle behind magical dolls called **poppets.** Whatever is done magically to the doll is done to the person on the receiving end of the magical spell. Sympathetic magic is the principle behind amulets and talismans, magically charged objects that bestow protection, healing, and even supernatural powers upon the person who wears or owns them.

that became the norm. Drawings of witches from earlier times show them wearing the clothing of their periods, including scarves and hats of different fashions. One possibility is that the witch's hat evolved from the Church's general disapproval of pointed hats, which it said were associated with the horns of the Devil. The Devil is often described as a black figure or a man dressed in black. Thus, a witch in black clothes and pointy black hat became a symbol for wickedness.

Modern witches look like ordinary people of all ages, both sexes, and different races. Many of them wear ceremonial robes in their rituals.

What about those brooms?

During the witch hunts, accused witches "confessed" to traveling through the air on brooms to their nighttime meetings. They left their houses through their chimneys. They also rode other common tools they were likely to own, such as pitchforks, poles, and shovels. Some even rode demons. These travels did not really take place, but because of the false confessions of some accused witches, people believed that they did.

Modern witches have adopted brooms as a magical tool and a symbol of their **Craft**.

Magical arts also involve divination, or telling the future, and the skilled use of herbs and plants. Early people discovered the medicinal and poisonous properties of plants. A magically empowered person knew how to combine them for special effect. Healing magic was especially important.

As supernatural forces became personified in the gods and goddesses of various mythologies, magical people sought their help, addressing them in prayers and in rituals.

Magic played an important role in ancient Egypt and was performed by priests. They were skilled in spell-casting, divination, **necromancy** (summoning the dead for divination), the making of amulets and talismans, the use of magical figures similar to poppets, and magic in medicine. They believed that spirits caused illnesses by invading the body and that they had to be driven out. The Egyptians developed systems of using magically charged names and words to command the right forces.

Magic also was important to the Babylonians, Assyrians, Hebrews, and the Greeks and Romans. These peoples saw the spirit world as teeming with beings that interfered with daily life. Magic could keep the spirits at bay. Organizations and rankings developed concerning the type of people who practiced certain kinds of magic. Handbooks of magic recipes were created. Laws regulating magic were passed.

Although magical people performed important services, the general population feared them. Witches, sorcerers, magicians—whatever they were called—were "outsiders." They were believed to act outrageously, do scandalous things, and defy society's norms. They could harm and even kill with a look called the **evil eye**. This fear of magic and magical people is found in all cultures, even tribal societies. Sometimes the magical people were hunted, arrested, and punished.

Christianity was born into a world brimming with magic. Belief in Jesus replaced people's need for magic. As Christianity spread and supplanted pagan religions, the magic practiced by pagans was suppressed and discouraged.

The Bible refers to witchcraft, though scholars have debated the accuracy of translations of the original Hebrew and Greek. The famous passage in Exodus 22:18, "Thou shalt not suffer a witch to live," is said by some scholars to refer to poisoners, not witches.[4] Others say it means witches or sorceresses in general. Passages like that came to have a terrible power about 1,000 years later, when a frenzy of witch hunting seized Europe for several hundred years.

In an increasingly Christian world, magic was pushed further and further to the edges of society. Eventually magic was outlawed, but centuries of traditional dependency on its power made it hard to eliminate. Folk magic, with herbs, plants, spells, amulets, and talismans, remained a staple of village life, even among Christian communities. The people who performed those services were called witches, cunning

Figure 1.1 *Satan marks a witch with his claw.* (R. P. Guaccius, *Compendium Maleficarum*, 1626)

men and cunning women, wise men and wise women, and many other names, including diviners, consulters with familiar spirits, wizards, necromancers, charmers, enchanters, Gypsies, exorcists, astrologers, numerologists, and even fortune-tellers. People continued to need and fear magic. And over time, the fear grew as the Christian Church increased pressure to stamp out pagan ways. When the church organized persecutions of heretics, witchcraft became linked to the Devil.

The notion that witches serve the Devil still exists today. Challenging those old stereotypes is a new brand of witchcraft that is an organized religion. Witchcraft, with a capital W, also called Wicca, has the same morals and ethics as Christianity but very different ways of worshiping. To complicate the picture, spell-casting witchcraft that is part of folk magic still exists, side by side with various religions, and with Wicca. This brand of witchcraft is not a religion, but is the survivor of very ancient practices.

One can be a witch without being a religious witch. It may seem confusing, but it hasn't stopped Wicca from becoming one of the fastest growing new religions in the West. Will Wicca change the popular definition of witchcraft? History is being made right now.

The Inquisition's Reign of Terror

St. Claude, France, 1598. No one is safe in the tiny village, located in Upper Jura, a region north of Lyon and near the Swiss border. St. Claude and the entire Jura area are under attack by witches. The most ruthless inquisitors in the service of the church are determined to fight them. Their mission: complete extermination.

Lives and entire families have already been erased. Any accusation of witchcraft brings arrest, torture, trial, and death at the hands of the authorities. People live in fear. The slightest wrong word to a neighbor can send them straight to the office of the Inquisition.

Little Loyse Maillat is only eight, but her parents say she is possessed by demons. How else to explain her convulsions and strange behavior? Priests agree. They have sent five demons out of her.

Afterward, Loyse says she has been cursed by a witch. She and her parents blame an old woman, Françoise Secretain, who has a spotless reputation. But Loyse has a story about how the old woman sent devils into her through food she ate.

One of the chief inquisitors is Henri Boguet, a man dedicated to killing witches at all costs. He has Secretain arrested and interrogated. Her protests of innocence fall on deaf ears. He knows she is guilty, and he will make her say so. By the time Boguet is done with her, she has confessed to causing Loyse to be possessed, killing people's cattle, attending witches' **sabbats** (festivals) and worshiping the Devil, and other abominable crimes.

Secretain is forced to name accomplices. She accuses many others. Boguet is pleased, for now he can launch a massive witch hunt. He sends Secretain to the stake to be burned alive, followed by many of the innocents she was forced to name.

PANIC OVER WITCHES

Hundreds and hundreds of trials like this took place all over Europe for several centuries. The most intense witch hunts were in the sixteenth century. Boguet was one of many inquisitors who believed that witches and the Devil were a serious threat. He showed no mercy to man, woman, or child if he thought them to be witches. He ordered children to be tortured, saying that even children were beyond help once they were in league with Satan.

Some of the witch hunts and trials exploded into mass persecutions. At about the same time that Boguet was scorching the Jura land in search of witches, another inquisitor, Peter Binsfeld, was laying waste in the Treves area of Germany. Binsfeld, Bishop of Treves, was instrumental in sending 306 people to be burned at the stake.

The Treves witch panic occurred between 1587 and 1594. Drought and diseased crops were blamed on witches. Binsfeld oversaw interrogation and torture, even of children. Over the course of the panic, more than 6,000 persons were accused of being witches. Prominent citizens were not immune. Even one of the chief trials judges was convicted of witchcraft and executed. So were two burgomasters (mayors), and several councilors and associate judges. Protestant clerics were ruined. Families of the convicted lost all their land, money, and possessions.

How did this hysteria happen? What caused people to believe that witches were everywhere, and that the only remedy was torture and death?

THE INQUISITION IS BORN

In its beginning, the Inquisition was not overly concerned about witches and witchcraft. The Inquisition was the Catholic Church's campaign against heretics. A heretic is a misbeliever. Heretics to Catholicism were other faiths, rival factions, and, as the net of the Inquisition widened, social outcasts and political enemies. In short, heretics were anyone or any organization that threatened the power and authority of the Church.

One thousand years after the life of Jesus, Christianity was still struggling for dominance in the European world. Powerful sects such as the Albigenses, Waldenses, and Cathars competed with Christianity for followers. In the East, Islam was gaining strength and invading Christian turf. In 1086 Pope Urban II launched the first Crusades to fight the infidels in the Holy Land.

The Crusades absorbed men, money, and time, and made it difficult for the Church to fight heretics closer to home. In 1184 Pope Lucius III issued a papal bull—a command—to bishops to "make inquisition," or investigate, all heretics. No serious campaign began, however, until Pope Gregory IX, who ruled from 1227 to 1233. Gregory invited Franciscan monks to undertake inquisitions, and he issued two bulls authorizing Dominican monks to do the same.

The Inquisition's first major victims were the Order of the Knights Templar, who were important to the Crusades, but arrogant in their wealth and power, so much so that the Order threatened kings. Philip IV of France, who owed large sums to the Knights, pressured the Church to act against the Order. The charges of heresy included accusations of devil worship. The charges were false but were enough to destroy the Order. The knights were burned at the stake. Burning was considered the most effective way to destroy heretics and discourage others from heresy. Sometimes the convicted were hanged.

Over time inquisitors gained increasing power and ways to persecute the Church's enemies. By the fourteenth century they had the power to arrest, torture, and try accused witches.

Meanwhile, superstitious fears of sorcery and witchcraft were increasing in the general population. Folk magic and spell-casting were part of daily life. Anything that went wrong was blamed on evil spells.

Figure 2.1 *Jaques de Molay (1243–1314), the last Grand Master of the Knights Templar, burns at the stake and shakes his fist at his executioner.* (Bettmann/Corbis)

For example, crop failures were blamed on **blasting**, a malicious act of destruction attributed to witches.

Every village had at least one or two persons who were skilled in herbal lore and folk magic. They were consulted for blessings and protection—and also for revenge.

Fears about witchcraft became a weapon for the Inquisition. In 1484 Pope Innocent VIII authorized inquisitors to use witchcraft as a charge of heresy. The church argued that witches, by default, were in league with the Devil.

Suddenly the job of the inquisitor became much easier. No longer did he have to prove religious deviation. All he had to do to destroy an enemy was torture him or her into confessing witchcraft. It was the perfect heresy.

Not everyone targeted by the Inquisition was accused of witchcraft. For example, the astronomer Galileo (1564-1642) insisted that the earth revolves around the sun, not vice versa, which earned him the attention of the Inquisition. He was sentenced to house arrest.

The Inquisition raged for several centuries. The Protestant Reformation, declared in 1517 by Martin Luther, added fuel to the fire, because Protestants were included in the list of enemies. In turn Protestants did their share of persecutions and burnings in just as ruthless a fashion as the Catholics.

Witch hunts were most intense in Germany, Switzerland, parts of France, and the Low Countries (modern-day Belgium and the Netherlands). There also was significant activity in Scandinavia, Italy, Spain, and Portugal. The Spanish Inquisition was even exported to the New World, with an office established in Mexico.

Witch hunts swept through Britain and Scotland, though most witches there were hanged and not burned. The hysteria touched the American colonies, too, leading to sensational trials in Salem, Massachusetts, in 1692.

The Witch Finder Generall

In seventeenth-century England Matthew Hopkins, the son of a minister, was an opportunist looking for fame and a fast pound. At the time the witch hysteria was gripping the country. Hopkins resolved to become the most famous witch finder England ever saw, even though he knew next to nothing about witchcraft.

Hopkins skimmed King James I's famous *Daemonologie,* a guide to the ways of witches, to learn enough to sound informed. He recruited an accomplice, John Stearne.

In 1645 Hopkins announced that the town of Manningtree, where he lived and practiced law, was brimming with witches. They had tried to kill him. Now he was compelled to drop his law practice and go after them and bring them to justice.

Hopkins billed himself as "The Witch Finder Generall" and made up the story that Parliament had appointed him to rid the countryside of witches. He said he possessed a secret "Devil's List" of the code names of all the witches in England.

Hopkins and Stearne went from town to town, scooping up gossip and making accusations of witchcraft. Most of the charges were of bewitching people and their livestock to death; causing illness and lameness; having pacts with the Devil; and entertaining evil spirits such as familiars, which usually were nothing more than household pets.

The accused would be arrested, and Hopkins would torture them into confessions. The use of torture was forbidden in England, but officials looked the other way while it was done. Hopkins had a mean streak, and his tortures were often extreme. He beat and starved his victims. He pricked them with needles. He deprived them of sleep and made them walk in the cells until their feet were blistered. He especially liked to "swim" victims. They would be bound hand and foot and tossed into deep water. If they floated, they were guilty. If they sank, they were innocent. Sinkers usually drowned.

Figure 2.2 *Witches accused by Matthew Hopkins name their familiars.*
(Fortean Picture Library)

(continues)

(continued)

In Chelmsford, Hopkins caused 17 people to be hanged, and several to die in jail. In Bury St. Edmonds, 124 people were brought to trial, and 68 of them were hanged. In all, Hopkins was responsible for the executions of 230 people, and the arrests and tortures of hundreds more. To make matters worse he charged outrageous fees.

His moment of fame and glory was short. Within a year there was a serious backlash against him and his tactics. By 1647 he and Stearne went their separate ways. Hopkins vanished from sight. According to Stearne, Hopkins fell ill with consumption (tuberculosis) and died at his home in Manningtree.

Records exist of his burial at the Mistley churchyard, but no tombstone with his name on it has ever been found. Hopkins' ghost is said to haunt the pond.

WANTED: INQUISITORS

As the Inquisition expanded, the church needed more and more inquisitors. "Inquisitor" had a job description. The candidate was at least 40 years old, for maturity was important. He was a forceful preacher and "full of zeal" for his task. He was fair and even-handed, but not moved by pitiful displays of emotion and begging for mercy.

In actuality many inquisitors were cruel and cold. They felt no sympathy for the sufferings of their victims and the lives they ruined. They could watch people be subjected to tortures that were worse than death itself, and at the end of the day, feel they were doing God's work.

The inquisitors had plenty of help from others, for there was money to be made in killing people. Judges, jailers, police, executioners, and informants made money. State and church treasuries were enriched.

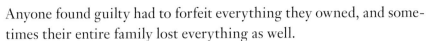

Anyone found guilty had to forfeit everything they owned, and some-times their entire family lost everything as well.

In Britain witch hunting was done mostly by Anglicans rather than Catholics. King Henry VIII broke the power of the Catholic Church there in 1536. "Witch finders" were opportunists who earned their living from exposing witches. They were paid a fee by towns and vil-lages for every witch executed.

HANDBOOKS

Inquisitors wrote their own handbooks on how to treat their victims. Some of the handbooks focused on witches, such as the *Malleus Ma-leficarum*, written in 1486 by two Dominicans, Heinrich Kramer and Jacob Sprenger.

The handbooks described the characteristics of witches and the evil things they were supposed to do. According to the handbooks, witches were thoroughly wicked and did nothing but harm people and animals. They made pacts, or agreements, with the Devil, who gave them demons in the forms of animals to do their bidding, called **familiars** or **imps**. They attended foul celebrations called sabbats, where they danced, ate roasted babies, trampled and spit on the cross, and praised the Devil. They had orgies. They caused people to become possessed by demons.

Where the evidence ever came from for these wild tales is not known. There is no historical evidence to back up any of the claims in these handbooks about sabbats and devil-worshiping **covens**.[1] But inquisitors tortured people into confessions that matched the claims in their handbooks.

There were a few voices of reason, skeptics who argued that such claims could not possibly be true. Witches did not shape-shift into an-imals, fly about on brooms or the backs of demons, or kiss the Devil's hind end. They did not snatch babies, roast them, and eat them.

For centuries the skeptics were outnumbered. People believed the inquisitors.

CASUALTIES

The Inquisition finally ended in the 1700s. It was halted by backlash against the campaigns and by political and social reforms and changes. In England, for example, a new Witchcraft Act was passed in 1735 that removed the death penalty for witchcraft, sorcery, enchantment, and conjuration, though those remained crimes of fraud.

No one knows exactly how many people died in the Inquisition. Some records were poorly kept, and not all survive. Historians estimate that several hundred thousand people were victims.[2] Most were women, but many men died, too, and so did children of both sexes. Even dogs were tried and executed as heretics.

Modern Witches call the Inquisition "the Burning Times." Some have said that 9 million witches died, but that figure is considered by historians to be too high.

In 1998 Pope John Paul II commissioned 50 scholars to go through Vatican records and issue a report on the Inquisition. In 2000 he issued an apology for "errors committed in the service of the truth through the recourse of non-evangelical methods." In other words the pope apologized for one of the worst campaigns of terror in history.

Anatomy of a Witch Trial and Execution

John Fian is a handsome young schoolmaster in Saltpans, Scotland, in the late sixteenth century. More than one young lass in the area fancies herself in a romance with him. There is also an air of mystery about him, for it is rumored in the village that he is a bit of a conjurer and practices magical arts. No one thinks much about it—until a servant girl accuses him of witchcraft in 1590.

The rest of Fian's life is a nightmare of unspeakable torture, followed by an excruciating death by being maimed, strangled, and then cast on a fire. Others are burned along with him in what become Scotland's most infamous witch trials and most brutal tortures.

Fian and his accused accomplices, known as the North Berwick Witches, were unlucky to live during one of the worst times of witch hunting. Not even a village in Scotland was too remote for the witch panic. King James VI, who held the Scottish throne at that time, was as committed to killing witches as were the religious inquisitors who stalked Europe.[1]

The girl who accused Fian of witchcraft was suspected of being a witch herself and was tortured to name others. That was how justice was pursued then: Guilt was assumed, torture was applied to coerce the accused to name others—anybody—and protests of innocence were ignored.

The trials of Fian and the North Berwick Witches were duplicated over and over again in similar cases in other countries. Once accusations were made and torture began, the victims fell like dominoes. Truth had little meaning.

SEEDS OF DISASTER

The North Berwick tragedy began with Gillis Duncan, a maid who worked for a man named David Seaton in the town of Tranent, Scotland. In 1590 Duncan suddenly underwent a marked change in personality and behavior. She acquired an unexplained ability to heal, and she took to sneaking out of the house at night.

Seaton demanded to know what was going on. Duncan could give him no satisfactory answers. In all likelihood she was sneaking out to meet a secret lover. She may also have had a natural healing gift all along and for some reason started to use it then.

At any rate, Seaton was convinced that these changes in his maid were the work of the Devil. She denied it, so he had her tortured. Her fingers were crushed in a vice called the *pilliwinks*. Her head was *thrawed*, that is, tied with a rope that was twisted and yanked violently back and forth.

Amazingly, Duncan held to her denial. This meant to others that the Devil was helping her resist, so she was tortured some more. The next step was to look for the proof that could not be denied, the "Devil's mark," also called the "witch's mark." According to inquisitors, the Devil put a mark on the body of his servants.[2] Victims had their bodies searched for any mark, such as a mole, wart, birthmark, or blemish. If none were visible, their entire bodies were shaved of hair.

Rare was the accused witch who had no mark. If no marks were found, it didn't matter. Inquisitors claimed that the Devil made his marks invisible or caused the marks to disappear to confound the judges.[3] A mark was found on Duncan. Knowing there was no hope for her now, she broke down and confessed to having a pact with the Devil. She was thrown in jail and forced to name accomplices.

Besides Fian, Duncan named Agnes Sampson, an old and well-respected woman who lived in Haddington, and Euphemia Maclean and Barbara Napier, two well-respected women of Edinburgh. There were other men and women, too, but those were the principal ones. According to Duncan, Sampson had tried to bewitch her husband to death, and Napier had used witchcraft to kill her husband, an earl.

All those Duncan accused were arrested. King James and a council of noblemen oversaw their interrogation and torture.

Figure 3.1 *The North Berwick witches plead their innocence before the judges, including King James VI (seated).* (Fortean Picture Library)

TREATMENT OF ACCUSED WITCHES

When a person was accused of witchcraft, officials encouraged witnesses to come forward and testify against the accused. If someone had grudges to be repaid, this was a good time to do it. Proof was not necessary.

Armed with accusations, the judges and inquisitors demanded confessions from the accused. Increasing torture was applied until the

The Last Witch on Trial

The last witch trial didn't occur hundreds of years ago. Amazingly, a woman in England was put on trial in the 1940s for being a witch. It was called the "trial of the century."

Helen Duncan was a medium, a person who has psychic ability, especially for communicating with the dead. Duncan's ability was natural from birth. She was born in Scotland in 1898 and had her first psychic experiences as a child. When she was older, she conducted seances. She married, moved to England, and had six children.

In earlier times open displays of psychic ability would have quickly branded someone a witch. In Duncan's time people had a better understanding of psychic ability, but many people were still frightened of it. England still had a law that made witchcraft a crime. The law had been revised several times in history, the last being 1735. In modern times the Witchcraft Act of 1735, as the law was called, was used to prosecute mediums for fraud.

In 1933 Duncan was charged with fraud and was tried in Edinburgh. She was convicted, but it did not stop her from working as a medium. After the start of World War II, many people came to her to try to communicate with loved ones who had been killed. In 1941 Duncan had a psychic vision that changed her life for the worse. She saw a dead sailor from a battleship named the HMS *Barham*.

court was satisfied. In the absence of specific acts of witchcraft, the court could accuse victims of pacts with the Devil, attending sabbats, having familiars, and other things impossible for victims to disprove.

Many accused withstood unbelievable levels of torture, even knowing they were doomed to die. Convictions meant that their families would lose all of their possessions to the state. Everything they had worked for and inherited would be confiscated, leaving

Duncan did not know that the British government was keeping a secret that the *Barham* had been sunk off the coast of Malta. Not even members of the sailors' families knew. The government was afraid that the loss would bring the country's morale down.

Duncan's vision convinced government officials that she must be a spy rather than a medium. They worried that she would reveal other secrets—such as the plans for D Day, the invasion of France planned by the Allies to make a powerful strike against Germany.

The government watched Duncan for two years, and then charged her with witchcraft under the 1735 law. She was brought to trial in 1944 in London. At least 40 people testified on her behalf, but the government called her a "pest." She was convicted and sent to prison for nine months. Duncan protested her innocence and said that lies had been told about her.

Duncan's conviction angered Britain Prime Minister Winston Churchill. He demanded an explanation. Embarrassed, Parliament repealed the 1735 Witchcraft Act in 1951.

After her release from prison, Duncan resumed her mediumship, but her career and her health were ruined. Opponents and police harassed her. She returned to Scotland, where she died in 1956. Duncan's supporters have tried to get the government to officially clear her name but without success. She remains the last witch tried under English law.

surviving family members with nothing. In addition their families would be shamed, perhaps even cast out of society.

For some victims denial was a matter of religious faith and personal honor. They could not bear to confess to vile crimes they did not commit or would not ever even think of doing.

FALL OF THE WOMEN

In the North Berwick trials, Sampson accumulated 53 charges against her. Her body was shaved and a Devil's mark was found. Old and frail, she was pinned to a dirty, cold jail cell wall by a witch's bridle. It was like a horse bridle made for people, and it had four sharp prongs that cut into the cheeks and tongue. Sampson's head was thrawed, and she

Figure 3.2 *Satan lures the North Berwick witches to indulge in evil practices, such as causing shipwrecks by casting spells.* (Fortean Picture Library)

was deprived of sleep. Finally she could stand no more, and she confessed to all charges.

She agreed that she and 100 witches had attended sabbats, danced, and kissed the Devil's behind. She and the other accused witches had tried to murder King James and his Danish bride by raising storms at sea in an attempt to sink their ship when they traveled from Denmark to Scotland. And, she had used toad venom to **hex** the king and cause him great pain.

Sampson's confessions only secured her doom. She was burned in January 1591. She was granted the mercy of being strangled to death first before being tossed into the fire.

Maclean, the daughter of a lord and the wife of a wealthy man, hired six lawyers to defend her, to no avail. She was convicted of attempted murder by witchcraft and was burned on July 25, 1591. Her lands were forfeited to King James.

Napier was convicted as well but pleaded pregnancy. Sometimes courts were lenient on pregnant women, sentencing them to jail instead of death. Napier was jailed and eventually freed.

FIAN'S PAINFUL JOURNEY TO DEATH

The worst tortures were done to Fian, who was charged with 20 counts of witchcraft and high treason for attempting to murder the king and his bride by drowning. Among the other charges were

- acting as Satan's secretary during coven meetings
- making a pact with Satan and kissing his behind
- bewitching people, including a rival in love
- seducing women by witchcraft
- bewitching animals
- robbing graves to steal corpses and body parts for magical charms
- breaking into a church to allow the Devil to lead an infernal service and preach from the pulpit

Like Sampson, Fian indignantly denied these charges at first. His head was thrawed severely, and still he denied. King James ordered what he called "the most severe and cruel pain in the world," the "boots." This was a vise that fit from knees to ankles and was progressively tightened with blows from a hammer. Fian was given three blows.

Pins were stabbed into his tongue. His interrogators claimed that the Devil had done it to prevent Fian from talking.

Broken, Fian confessed in writing and renounced the Devil. He vowed to live as a good Christian.

The following day, the jailers claimed that Fian said he had been visited by the Devil in the night to demand he remain in service to him. The Devil reminded him that he had sold his soul. It is not certain whether the jailers made this up, or whether Fian was delirious from his torture.

Fian managed to break out of jail and flee to Saltpans. The King's men found him and returned him to jail. His body was shaved, but no Devil's mark was found. Enraged, James was determined to get another confession out of Fian that he had renewed his pact with the Devil.

All of Fian's fingernails were ripped off with pincers called a *turkas*. The exposed nail beds were stabbed with two needles each. Fian did not confess. He was put back in the boots and hammered so many times that his lower legs were completely crushed. Blood and bone marrow spurted from the wounds. There would be no more escapes for Fian—or even walking. His legs were useless.

Still he would not confess. By then, he was probably in so much pain that he was barely conscious, let alone of sound mind. King James was livid. He had Fian thrown in a cart and taken to a hill in Edinburgh where a great bonfire was built. Fian was strangled and thrown immediately into the flames.

In all, 70 witches were tried in the North Berwick trials from 1590-91. Surviving records do not indicate how many were executed.

Trials like these were turned into great public spectacles, as a lesson to people. Imagine the fear they created. People lived under a terrible shadow, knowing they could be falsely accused of witchcraft at any time and that they had little or no hope of salvation if it happened. Another 100 to 150 years would pass before the witch hunts came to an end. Many thousands more would die.

Witchcraft in Early America

In the rocky hills near Easton, Pennsylvania, Peter Saylor is a man of mystery. He has the "power," something he inherited from his father, Johann Seiler, who immigrated to the colonies from Germany in 1738. Like his father, Peter can cure and curse. He can charm locks open and make poisonous snakes dance. His power is real, as most who live in the area know firsthand.

Every day, a steady stream of people seek out Saylor (who changed the spelling of his last name) to help them with their misery and needs. They believe that his magic is better than any medical help from a trained doctor.

Today, a 14-year-old neighbor girl comes to ask him to get rid of warts on her right hand. She has waited until the right day—the first Friday after a full moon, when the "power" is at its peak. Saylor cuts a raw potato in half. He rubs a cut side of one-half on the wart, and mutters strange words that the girl cannot hear well enough to understand. When he is done, he tells her to bury the potato in her yard. When it rots, the warts will be gone.

She is confident of the cure. It's not in the potato—she tried that herself and it didn't work. The cure is in the mystery of Peter Saylor's power.

After the girl, a farmer comes who is upset about his cattle. Several have sickened, and he fears that they have been bewitched. Saylor thinks for a moment, and then announces the name of the person who put a spell on the cattle. The farmer nods; it is a neighbor with whom he had an argument. Saylor mutters a prayer in a voice too low to be understood. He writes a magical charm or inscription on a piece of paper. He instructs the farmer to put it in the cattle's feed, and says they will soon be relieved.

And so it goes, day after day. Some people travel many miles and endure long waits to see Saylor. There are no official fees for his help—it's traditional for people like him to work for donations. His clients go away happy—and they pay him handsomely.

POWWOWERS

Witches came to America with the first settlers from England and Europe. They were not always called "witches," and they certainly were not the devil worshipers described by the Inquisition. But they practiced magic and folk healing, and they were powerful people in their towns and villages. Two of the strongest traditions were the **powwowers** and the power doctors, who healed physical and spiritual ailments.

The Saylor family is an example of powwowers, healers who mixed herbal lore, folk magic, Christian prayer, and a natural healing ability. The first powwowers were German immigrants, many of whom settled in Pennsylvania, West Virginia, and eastern Ohio. In Pennsylvania they became known as the Pennsylvania Dutch. The "Dutch" came from *Deutsch*, a German word meaning "German."

Their healing tradition was inherited and based on long traditions from their German homeland. No one knows when or why the immigrant healers became known as powwowers, a term borrowed from the Indians. Back home in Germany, such a healer was called a *braucher*, and if he dabbled in black magic, he was called a *hexenmeister*, a master of hexes or spells. They filled needs when doctors were not available, curing ailments, healing wounds, and protecting against the evils of the world.[1]

Johann Seiler, Peter's father, was among the first immigrants to be called a powwower. He was so successful that by 1779 he owned 200 acres of land, and continued to buy more. He treated both whites and Indians. The Indians called him "the great powwow man."

Seiler had 10 children, some of whom followed in his healing footsteps. The star of the family was Peter, the youngest son. Peter excelled in the ability to cast out illness. It was said that he sent illness into a nearby spooky hill called the Hexenkopf, or Witch's Head. The top of the hill has a rocky outcrop that, from certain angles, resembles a head. Locals feared the Hexenkopf, because witches were supposed to gather there at night for their revelries.

Powwowers could be either male or female, but most were men. Their secret arts were passed down from parent to child and involved herbal knowledge, incantations, and rituals. In a typical ritual, the powwower started by learning the name and nature of a person's complaint. This enabled him to concentrate on the problem. He made motions and passes with his hands, blew on the patient, or rubbed his own spit on a wounded or diseased part of the patient's body. While he did so, he recited certain prayers and incantations in a very low voice, in order to keep them secret. He might use props, such as potatoes, eggs, and string tied in knots. He often sent the patient home with instructions to follow that would complete the healing or lift a curse.

MOUNTAIN MARY

Though most powwowers were men, one of the most famous of them all was a woman, Mountain Mary. She was born Anna Maria Jungin in Germany and came to Philadelphia with her family just before the American Revolution. She was either engaged or married to a man named Theodore Benz, who was killed in the war.

Mary Young, as she called herself, never married after Theodore's death. Instead, she became a hermit in the Oley Hills in eastern Berks County, and became steeped in the magic of herbs and roots. She read the Bible and spent much time in prayer. Whether she honed skills inherited from her family or taught herself everything from scratch is not known.

Mary's reputation as a powwower spread far and wide. She was credited with miraculous cures. She was so popular that poems and ballads were written about her. She died in 1819 at the age of 70.

MAGICAL BOOKS

Mary had no textbooks, but most powwowers had certain magical books to aid them in their work. Some of the books were handwritten family dairies brought over from the Old Country. There were two books that were must haves, the bibles of powwowing.

One of them was *Sixth and Seventh Books of Moses*, a single book of spells and conjurations. The text was supposedly written by Johann Scheibel of Stuttgart, Germany, and was published after his death in 1849. It was said to be based upon the magic of the ancient Hebrews, lore dictated by God to Moses that was too powerful to be included in the Bible. Instead, the lore was passed down orally from father to son, including to the legendary and magically powerful King Solomon.

The *Sixth and Seventh Books of Moses* contains more than 125 magic circles, seals, talismans, and *hexenfoos* for summoning spirits and working spells. The *hexenfoos* are symbols that protect against evil and bewitchment. Most are six-pointed flowers and five-pointed stars drawn within circles. They were drawn on barns, for example, to protect animals. They were drawn on the ground as magic circles. The powwower stood in the middle to call down his power for spell-casting.

According to folk tales from Germany, the *Sixth and Seventh Books of Moses* is dangerous if it falls into the wrong hands or is misused.

The most important magical book of all in powwow tradition was *Long Lost Friend*, by John George Hohman, who left Hamburg, Germany, for Philadelphia in 1802.[2] Like members of the Seiler/Saylor family, Hohman had a natural gift for healing and an interest in folk medicine and magical spells. By 1815 he and his family were settled near the Hexenkopf, and Hohman was gaining a reputation for healing, though he seems to have never called himself a powwower.

He published *Long Lost Friend* in 1820. It contains dozens of "arts and remedies" for humans and animals: curing ailments, preventing and curing bewitchment, and protection against robbery and violence. Mixed with the superstition and herbal lore are charms, inscriptions, incantations, and "little prayers" of a Christian nature. *Long Lost Friend* is still in print today.

Hohman's book quickly became *the* book among powwowers. It was so powerful in its own right that just to own a copy brought power. Hex doctors worked black magic with it. The Saylor family placed great importance upon it. The book was so important that in the early twentieth century, a murder was committed over it.

HEX MURDER

John Blymire was born in 1895 in York County, Pennsylvania, to a family of skilled powwowers. Little John inherited some ability but never achieved the talent of his father and grandfather. Misfortune and illness seemed to follow him around.

By 1912 Blymire had become convinced that all of his troubles were caused by a hex someone had put on him. According to tradition a hex cannot be broken unless the identity of the hexer is discovered. Blymire spent years consulting dozens of powwowers without success.

Finally, in 1928, he consulted a woman powwower, who told him the hexer was a man named Nelson Rehmeyer, a rival powwower who was rumored to be able to conjure up the demon Beelzebub. The curse on Blymire could be broken if he obtained Rehmeyer's copy of the *Long Lost Friend* and burned it, or else cut a lock of Rehmeyer's hair and buried it six to eight feet deep in the ground.

Blymire took two men and went to see the rival witch. He demanded that Rehmeyer give him the spell book. Rehmeyer refused and fought—and was killed.

Blymire and his accomplices were arrested. In a sensational trial, they were convicted, Blymire and one man of first degree murder, and the second accomplice of second degree murder. Blymire was sentenced to life in prison. He served 23 years and five months. He was released in 1953 at age 58. He took a job as a janitor, his powwowing days long over.

Native American Witches

Witchcraft beliefs are present in all cultures. Before white settlers came to North America, Native Americans had their own beliefs about witches and sorcerers. Many of the beliefs were similar to those of Europeans.

Witches—who could be either men or women—were associated with evil spells and magic. They had the power to shape-shift, fly through the air, bewitch, and curse. They used dolls for spell-casting. They possessed the evil eye, causing people and animals to have bad luck, fall ill, or die.

As immigrants moved into Native American territories and cultures mixed, some of the European beliefs were absorbed into Native American witchcraft lore.

White settlers feared Native American witches just as they did the ones they left behind in Europe. In the sixteenth century Spaniards who controlled large portions of what is now New Mexico were especially fearful of a Mexican Indian woman, Beatriz de Los Angeles, and her daughter, Juana de la Cruz, who were famous in the Santa Fe area for their witchcraft powers. Stories about them told of their many poisonings and death hexes. Daughter Juana was said to fly about at night in an egg and spy on people, especially her lovers. If she caught them being unfaithful, she fed them enchanted milk that killed them.

The supposed powers of these witches worried Spanish officials, who had the women arrested and taken to the Inquisition in Mexico City. No direct evidence could be found against them, however, so they were set free. In Europe they probably would have been tortured into confessions and executed.

Powwowing is still practiced today, and is sometimes combined with other techniques, such as Reiki, a form of energy healing.

POWER DOCTORS

Similar to the powwowers are the power doctors, backwoods healers, and spell-casters of the Ozarks Mountains. Power doctors must learn their skill from someone who is not a blood relative. They can teach their art only to two or three others; otherwise, the power will be lost. They also work for donations, not for set fees.

There are no central magical books for power doctors like those for powwowers. Rather, the power doctors learn hundreds of recipes and spells. Many of their spells and charms are based on Christian prayers. Some incantations are nonsense, such as "bozz bozzer mozz mozzer kozz kozzer."

Power doctoring is a declining art, replaced by newer and more modern healing techniques.

DIABOLIC WITCHCRAFT

Some of the earliest settlers in America viewed witchcraft not as a folk healing art but as something far more deadly. In New England, as well as in some of the other original colonies, immigrants brought European beliefs about witches as servants of the Devil. Some of these beliefs were tied into strict and conservative

Figure 4.1 *An engraved portrait of Cotton Mather, a Boston Congregationalist minister and writer whose works include a commentary on the Salem witch trials.* (Bettmann/ Corbis)

religious practices, such as those of the Puritans, who came to Massachusetts.

Preachers like Increase Mather and his son, Cotton Mather, believed that people were under a constant threat by the Devil and his witches. Any problem, whether personal, social, or political, was caused by demonic interference. The Mathers agreed with demonologists in England and Europe that witches were a threat, and people were vulnerable because they were not strict enough in their religious practice. They preached sermons about the dangers of witches. Cotton Mather investigated cases of possession, which he blamed on witches.

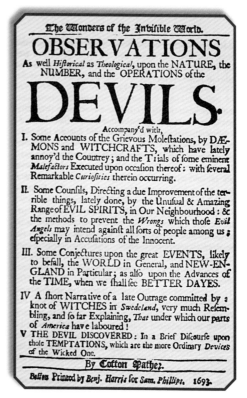

Figure 4.2 *Title page of Cotton Mather's* The Wonders of the Invisible World. *The book condemns witchcraft as an evil magical power.* (Stapleton Collection/Corbis)

In the 1660s witchcraft trials took place in the colonies, and accused witches were punished and executed. Some of the accused were probably innocent, like many of the victims in Europe and England. Some were like the powwowers and power doctors, people who practiced folk magic and medicine. Increase Mather supported the witch trials. The Devil, he said, was out to destroy communities.

His beliefs were echoed by Cotton, born in 1663. Fears over diabolic witchcraft increased, especially in Massachusetts. By 1692 the witchcraft tension was ready to explode. It did, in Salem.

Witchcraze in Salem

Today they would just be kids having some fun with divination and witchy games. But seventeenth-century Massachusetts was a time and place steeped in political and social unrest—and a deep fear of witchcraft. The girls in Salem Village amusing themselves to pass the time during a cold winter had no idea they would set off the worst witch hunt in American history. People were ruined. People died. People were cursed. And it all started with innocent games.

In the winter of 1691-92, Elizabeth (Betty) Parris and her 11-year-old cousin, Abigail Williams, were quite the envy of other girls in town. Their nanny was a foreign woman who knew mysterious things and powers. Tituba Indian was a slave from Barbados, as was her husband, John. Betty's father, Reverend Samuel Parris, had purchased them when he worked as a merchant in Barbados. "Indian" was not their real last name, but a name given to them to describe their race.

To the girls, Tituba was an exciting woman. And, she was willing to share some of her magical secrets with them. The winters in Salem were long, hard, and boring. Tituba told stories about her native Barbados and taught the girls how to look into the future.

Betty and Abigail invited some of their friends to learn the secrets, too—Susannah Sheldon, Elizabeth Booth, Elizabeth Hubbard, Mary Warren, Sarah Churchill, Mercy Lewis, and Ann Putnam Jr. Soon they had divination parties going. After all, what girl doesn't want to know if she will marry, who will be her husband, and what the fates have in store for her.

Tituba showed the girls how to make a **scrying** tool by floating an egg white in a glass of water. (*Scrying* means gazing into a reflective surface to see the future.) The tool was a crude crystal ball. The egg white would take different shapes in answer to questions. The girls took turns reading fortunes for each other. It was all great fun—until one of them said she saw a coffin in the egg white. Suddenly the fortune telling wasn't fun anymore. It was scary and creepy. The girls were never the same again.

In January 1692 Betty Parris began having hysterical fits. She would crawl into bed and make strange, animal-like noises. Her fits were contagious, and soon Elizabeth Hubbbard began having them. It is not known whether the girls thought they were genuinely possessed, or whether they were trying to cover up their involvement in Tituba's magic. Either way, Salem Village exploded.

Reverend Parris was alarmed. Such behavior could only be explained as bewitchment by an evil witch. He had three doctors examine the girls. They all made the same diagnosis: Witchcraft! There was only one course of action: Identify the witch or witches, and get rid of her or them—by execution if necessary. The people of Salem Village agreed.

WHAT MADE SALEM READY TO HUNT WITCHES

The witch hysterias that gripped Europe and England in the seventeenth century had infected Colonial America, too. In New England the rigid Puritans were always on guard against the Devil and his servants. Preachers thundered from their pulpits about the traps laid by witches and the harm they could do. People who were suspected of witchcraft were sometimes tried. In some cases they were banished from a town. Sometimes they were hung.

New England was a hotbed of political and social rivalries. It was a climate ripe for witch hunting. Just like in Europe and England, any rival or disliked person could be charged with witchcraft. It was a good and righteous way to get rid of troublemakers.

Salem Village had its own peculiar politics. Named after the Hebrew word for peace, *shalom*, Salem Village was far from peaceful. The village was mostly controlled by Salem Town. Growing tensions had split the village in two: people who wanted to separate from the Town, and people who were content with the status quo. As Reverend, Parris had the difficult task of trying to hold the community together. Personally, he sided with the separatists. These politics played an important role in the unfolding of the witch hysteria.[1] The opportunity to get rid of social and political enemies by accusing them of witchcraft could not be resisted.

THE HYSTERIA INCREASES

The Salem Village girls were pressed by authorities to identify the witches responsible for their bewitchment. They had no choice but to start naming people. Pointing the finger at someone was called "crying out."

The first person cried out against was Tituba. The girls also named two lower-class housewives, Goodwife, or Goody, Sarah Good and Sarah Osborne. None of the accused attended the village church, and they indulged in scandalous behavior. Goody Good begged openly for money for her family, and Goody Osborne had allowed a servant to live under her roof—and then married him.

The three women were swiftly arrested and brought before Salem Town magistrates John Hathorne and Jonathan Corwin for questioning. The girls were present too—and fell into fits and swoons. They screamed that the witches roamed about town in the forms of spectral animals, and bit and pinched them. The two Sarahs protested their innocence. But Tituba, who had been beaten severely by Reverend Parris, confessed to be being a witch.

Her confession was shocking. Tituba said that a black dog—a familiar, or servant, of the Devil—had forced her to hurt the girls. Two large demonic cats, one black and one red, made her serve them. Tituba said she rode through the air on a pole to "witch meetings" with the two Sarahs. Their traveling companions were demon familiars. Sarah Good forced Tituba to hurt young Ann Putnam Jr. with a knife. Ann agreed, saying that the three witches had tried to cut off her head.

This tale was amazing enough, but Tituba did not stop. There were more witches than the three of them—a whole coven. They were led by a demon or the Devil, who appeared in the form of a tall, white-haired man dressed entirely in black. This man had forced Tituba to sign his devil's book in blood. She had seen nine other names in the book.

Tituba's wild story sent more shock waves through Salem Village. Officials were more determined that ever to find all the witches and destroy them. Tituba and the two Sarahs were sent to jail and put in heavy chains, which, people believed, would prevent them from wandering about in spectral form. Frail Sarah Osborne could not stand the harsh conditions and died there.

MORE WITCHES ARE EXPOSED

With the entire village in an uproar and people ready to believe in witches at the mention of a name, shrewd people saw opportunities to strike out against those they disliked. Ann Putnam Jr. was pressured by her mother to cry out against Martha Corey, wife of Giles Corey. In her fits, young Ann said she saw a vision of Martha's specter roasting a man over a fire. Other girls embellished this vision to include other witches and a devil's book.

Brought into court, Martha maintained her innocence. But her every word and gesture was mimicked by the girls, who claimed Martha was tormenting them in spirit. Even her own husband, Giles, testified against her.

A dangerous turning point was reached when one of the most re-spected women in the community, Rebecca Nurse, was accused by Ann Putnam Sr. Nurse had a spotless reputation, and had cooler heads prevailed, the entire hysteria might have stopped right there. But the mean-spirited Putnam said both Nurse and Martha Corey were pres-suring her to sign the devil's book, and Nurse had beaten Ann Jr. So, off to jail Nurse went.

With the fall of Nurse, the girls then cried out against four-year-old Dorcas Good, daughter of Sarah Good. They claimed she was trained to be a witch by her mother.

Other victims were

- John and Elizabeth Proctor, tavern keepers who were opposed to the witch hunt
- Sarah Cloyce, the sister of Rebecca Nurse
- Mary Warren, the maid of Elizabeth Proctor
- Bridget Bishop, whose flashy clothing and drinking had scandalized the villagers for years
- Abigail Hobbs, who was mentally ill
- Giles Corey

By this time, the girls were claiming that the witches were drink-ing the blood of their victims. There seemed to be no end to the wild stories that others would believe.

More victims followed:

- Nehemiah Abbot, an old man
- William and Deliverance Hobbs, the parents of Abigail Hobbs
- Edward Bishop, stepson of Bridget Bishop, and his wife Sarah
- Mary Esty, sister of Rebecca Nurse
- Mary Black, a black slave
- Sarah Wilds

(continues on page 58)

Blood on Their Hands

Condemned at Salem to die, Sarah Good was given one last chance by her accusers to repent as a witch. As she was led to the gallows, Good was urged by Reverend Richard Noyes to confess. Defiant, Good replied, "I am no more a witch than you are a wizard, and if you take away my life, God will give you blood to drink!" Her words were a curse, and the curse brought death and ruin for generations.

In 1717 Noyes did indeed have blood to drink—he choked to death on his own blood.

The curse also stuck to one of the magistrates who sent some of the accused to their deaths. Judge John Hathorne was a wealthy and respected man, part of a family involved in shipping and politics. Hathorne thoroughly believed in witchcraft and considered it a great evil. Though he posed skeptical questions at the trials, he was quite swayed by the flimsy evidence presented against the accused.

Hathorne never expressed any regret for his role in the trials and executions. But in the back of his mind, he surely must have worried about the curse leveled by Sarah Good. He also was openly hated by Philip English, whose wife Mary, was among the accused. Mary's health was so affected by her ordeal that she fell ill and died. Philip was shunned and lost his property and wealth. Hate is a curse, too.

From 1692 onward, the fortunes of the Hathorne family declined. They lost money, power, prestige, and social status. Family members blamed the curse. It was all Judge John's fault. He should have never participated in the trials.

The curse was still working more than a century later. Nathaniel Hawthorne was born in 1804 in Salem. Ironically his lineage included a marriage mingling the English and Hathorne families—the curser and the cursed united!

Young Nathaniel was fascinated by the legend of the curse, and worried how it would affect him, too. His ambition was to be a writer.

While in college he was persuaded by his sister to add a "w" to his surname. The "w" had been dropped generations before, but his sister felt that adding it back in would separate Nathaniel from his cursed ancestor.

Perhaps it did indeed help, for Nathaniel went on to become one of America's greatest writers of fiction. But he also publicly apologized for Judge Hathorne and his ancestors and asked for the curse to be lifted.

In the introduction to his first novel, *The Scarlet Letter* (1850), he stated:

> He [Judge Hathorne] made himself so conspicuous in the martyrdom of the witches, that their blood may fairly be said to have left a stain upon him... I know not whether these ancestors of mine bethought themselves to repent, and ask pardon of heaven for their cruelties... At all events, I, the present writer, as their representative, hereby take shame upon myself for their sakes, and pray that any curse incurred by them... may be now and henceforth removed.

Nathaniel also used the curse in the plot of his second novel, *The House of Seven Gables* (1851), a story based his own family history.

The fictional Pyncheon family suffers from inherited sin related to witchcraft. Judge Pyncheon uses the charge of witchcraft to execute a neighbor whose land he wants. The neighbor, Thomas Maule, curses him on the gallows: "Pyncheon, God will give you blood to drink and quench your greed for eternity."

Pyncheon gets the land and builds on it a grand house of seven gables. He chokes to death on his own blood at the housewarming party. The family fortunes slide. The curse ends when the land is restored to Maule's family.

Nathaniel used his own family home as the model for the house of seven gables. The house, located on Salem harbor, is one of the city's biggest tourist attractions and part of the city's witchcraft history.

(continued from page 55)

- Philip and Mary English
- Sarah Morey
- Lydia Dustin, who died in prison
- Susannah Martin
- Dorcas Hoar
- Reverend George Burroughs

The witch hunt spread even further to areas surrounding Salem Village.[2] You can see the terrible domino effect of one accusation leading to another. Burroughs especially was a target, for he had been minister of Salem Village before Parris, and had alienated many people.

TRIALS AND EXECUTIONS

By May 1692 Salem's jail was holding 100 accused witches. The village received a charter from the colony of Massachusetts to set up a court. It was called "Oyer and Terminer," which means "to hear and determine." Magistrates Hathorne and Corwin were joined by seven more men, including Lieutenant Governor William Stoughton, to begin trial proceedings. The famous father and son ministers, Increase and Cotton Mather, who were anti-witch zealots, were consulted about what to allow as evidence and testimony.

The judges were swift and harsh. They accepted the fits and spectral evidence of the girls, and began pronouncing the accused guilty and sentencing them to death. The first to be hanged was Bridget Bishop, on June 10. As a convicted witch, she could not be given a Christian burial. She was laid in a shallow grave on Gallows Hill, where hangings took place outside of the village. The same fate awaited others.

More executions swiftly followed. Some of the victims went meekly to their deaths, while others were outraged and defiant to the end. Sarah Good cursed one of the judges. Reverend Burroughs stunned onlookers by perfectly reciting the Lord's Prayer as he stood on the

Figure 5.1 *Painting of a scene from a Salem witch trial.* (Bettmann/Corbis)

gallows. It was commonly believed that a witch, a servant of the Devil, could not recite the Lord's Prayer without stumbling. But even this did not save the poor minister. Cotton Mather quickly stepped in and said the Devil was capable of even that as a clever trick. Burroughs was hanged, and his body was dumped in a shallow grave.

The hangings were gruesome enough, but the most spectacular execution was that of Giles Corey. Eighty years old and incapable of harming anyone, Corey refused to recognize the right of the court to try him. In punishment, he was taken out into a field, staked to the ground, and covered with a huge wooden plank. Then heavy stones were piled on top of him. Corey was pressed to death.

Of the 141 persons accused, 19 were hanged, and several died in prison. Some actually escaped conviction and managed to be acquitted, usually by confessing to being a witch. The convictions were big business, for the state was entitled to confiscate all of the money and property of the guilty.

Why did some of the victims choose to go to their deaths rather than confess to being a witch, and save their lives? Wouldn't the lie have been worth it? Not to people who lived at that time. Lying was considered one of the worst mortal sins that would condemn a soul to hell. At the very least, lying could make a person a social outcast. Today, there are more liberal attitudes toward lying, which may or may not be a good thing. The Puritans felt much differently about it.

THE HYSTERIA COMES TO AN END

Witch fever eventually cooled in Massachusetts, but not before the girls got completely out of hand. Carried away by the attention and success, they began crying out against famous people throughout the region. Prisons overflowed with the accused. Finally, colony Governor William Phips dissolved the Court of Oyer and Terminer, and made spectral evidence inadmissable.

THE AFTERMATH

Almost immediately, guilt set in.[3] Those on the prosecuting ends suffered mysterious illnesses and setbacks, as if they were being

Figure 5.2 *This bench, dedicated to Mary Parker, is part of the memorial erected in Salem for those who died during the Salem witchcraze.* (Art on File/Corbis)

punished for crimes against the innocent. Some of the judges expressed regret. Ann Putnam Jr. begged the community for forgiveness in 1706.

The witch trials sat like a huge stain upon the land for 300 years. In 1957 the legislature of Massachusetts passed a resolution exonerating some of the victims. Still, citizens felt they should do more.

In 1992 a memorial was erected to all the victims of the 1692 trial. It was dedicated by Elie Wiesel, a Nobel Laureate known for his work concerning the victims of Nazi concentration camps. The memorial is located at the Old Burying Point in Salem, and is a park-like square with stone benches engraved with the names of the victims.

The Old Religion Comes Out
of the Broom Closet

It's 1939 and Europe is on the brink of massive warfare, what will go down in history as the Holocaust, World War II. While the world's attention is focused on war, something else is happening deep in a forest in England: the initiation of a man who will become the most influential witch of the modern world.

Gerald B. Gardner has been invited to join a secret coven of witches in the New Forest. They are descendants from a long line of hereditary witches, practitioners of Witchcraft, the Old Religion.

They worship ancient gods, the Goddess, and her consort, the Horned God, who is not the Devil but a god of nature. They honor the seasonal changes of nature, practice magic, and conduct their mysterious rituals "**skyclad**," without clothing. They are keepers of ancient wisdom, the dwindling numbers of their kind who were nearly destroyed by the witch hunts of the Inquisition.

At least, that was the story according to Gardner years later as he enjoyed the spotlight of international fame. Gardner brought witchcraft out of the broom closet in 1956, and ever since then historians have tried to separate the fact from fancy in his life and claims. No doubt about it, there was plenty of fancy. Despite that, Gardner accomplished something no one else had done: He reinvented witchcraft as a religion.

Figure 6.1 *Monique Wilson and Gerald Gardner, who is credited with reinventing witchcraft as a religion.* (Fortean Picture Library)

Actually, Gardner was not the first person to view witchcraft as an organized religion. In the 1920s and 1930s, a British anthropologist, Margaret A. Murray, had made the argument that witchcraft was really a pagan Old Religion that predated Christianity. The witches persecuted by the inquisitors were practicing the remnants of pagan traditions, she said.

Murray called witchcraft the "Dianic cult" because of pagan worship of the goddess Diana. She said that for centuries witches had been organized in covens to practice their religion. People from every class and rank in society, even royalty, had been secret members.[1]

It was a glamorous idea, but there was a significant problem with it—it wasn't true. There was no historical evidence to back up Murray's claims. Decades passed, however, before Murray's ideas were finally laid to rest.[2]

In 1939, the year of Gardner's initiation, Murray's theory still held sway. But no witches dared come forward to talk about themselves, to agree or disagree with Murray, for witchcraft was still illegal in England—an old anti-witchcraft law from 1735 was still in effect. The law did not stop people from practicing folk magic, especially in rural areas—they were quiet about it. In 1951 the witchcraft law was repealed. For the first time in hundreds of years, witches in Britain could come out in the open without fear of landing in jail—at least for being a witch. Gardner seized the opportunity.

THE "FATHER" OF MODERN WITCHCRAFT

Prior to his turning professional Witch, Gardner had a varied career and an intense interest in magic and the occult. He was born, appropriately, on Friday the 13th in June 1884 to a well-to-do family in Blundellsands, near Liverpool, England. Later, Gardner claimed that one of his ancestors was Grissell Gairdner, who was burned as a witch in 1610 in Newburgh. And, his grandfather married a woman reputed to be a witch.

Gardner spent part of his early life in Ceylon, Borneo, and Malaysia. He started a career as a civil servant and worked in the Far East. In all of these places, he studied the local magical lore. He was interested in the history of Goddess worship and published a book on the subject, *A Goddess Arrives*, in 1939.

In 1936 Gardner, by then married, retired from civil service and returned to England, taking a home in the New Forest region. It didn't take him long to find people with similar interests in the occult. He became involved with the Fellowship of Crotona, a group of Co-Masons who ran "The First Rosicrucian Theater in England," which put on plays with occult themes.

The New Forest witches supposedly were a secret group within the fellowship. They claimed to be hereditary witches who practiced a craft passed down to them through the centuries. No one has ever been able to

Witch or Wiccan? What's in a Name?

Centuries ago, calling oneself a witch was an invitation to torture and a death sentence. Today, people who follow Witchcraft as a religion—with a capital "W"—are reclaiming the word as a badge of power and religious freedom.

Whether or not it will work and people will let go of old and strong concepts that witches are evil is an issue that is sometimes hotly debated among those who practice Witchcraft and other Neo-Pagan religions. On one side are those who say that "Witch" is the only right word, and on the other side are those who believe Witch ought to be replaced by "Wiccan."

The word "witch" comes from the Middle English word *witche*, which is derived from the Old English terms *wicca/'witt* (masculine), terms which refer to sorcerer and wizard, and *wicce/'witt* (feminine), which refers to sorceress and witch. The Indo-European root of these terms is *weik*, which has to do with magic and religion.

Wicche, a Middle English word, was later applied to both men and women. "Wizard" and "warlock" replaced it. *Wiche* described unpleasant old women in the fifteenth century. *Witch* first appeared in English in the sixteenth century.

Wica, with one "c," was first used by Gerald B. Gardner as the name of the religion of Witchcraft. He said it was given to him by the coven that initiated him. Alex Sanders added a second "c," making it *Wicca* in the 1960s.

Wicca has gained popularity and is preferred by some followers of the Craft because it doesn't carry all the "witches-are-evil" baggage from the past. But many other Witches believe that a witch by any other name is not the same.

document much about this coven.[3] Some historians think that Gardner made up stories about it later to give him authority as a Witch.

In the 1940s Gardner met Aleister Crowley, a famous English magician with a dark reputation. He also met other people who were important in British occult circles. He wrote a novel called *High Magic's Aid*, published in 1949, which included rituals.

Soon after the witchcraft law was repealed in 1951, Gardner broke away from the New Forest coven to establish his own. In 1953 he met Doreen Valiente, a woman interested in witchcraft, and initiated her. Valiente became Gardner's first and most important **high priestess**.

A year later Gardner published *Witchcraft Today*, his account of the history of witchcraft as an organized religion, and his own initiation into it. The book was a sensation.

Gardner told Valiente that he had inherited a "book of shadows" from the New Forest coven, a collection of rituals and lore supposedly passed down through centuries. Valiente found this book to be in poor shape. It was a jumble of fragments, folk lore, and **ceremonial magic** that bore the stamp of Aleister Crowley. From 1954 to 1957 Valiente helped Gardner rewrite the book. She removed most of the Crowley material and added poetic rituals celebrating the Goddess.

Gardner found himself in a media spotlight, and he thoroughly enjoyed it. Newspapers and tabloids clamored for information and photographs of naked witches doing their rituals. The claim that witches worshiped nude was probably made up by Gardner, but it played well to the media and a shocked public.

Figure 6.2 *British writer and occultist Aleister Crowley.* (Bettmann/Corbis)

In 1957 Valiente left Gardner's coven to pursue her own path as a witch. By then, covens were forming everywhere. Initiates still looked for "lineage," claims by covens that they descended from a long line of witches. Gardner initiated witches who went on to initiate others as well, among them Patricia Crowther, and Monique Wilson (Lady Olwen). The press dubbed them all "Gardnerian" witches.

Gardner published his last book, *The Meaning of Witchcraft*, in 1959. He died of a heart attack in 1964 while on a ship en route from Lebanon to England. He was buried in Tunis. His remains were later brought back to England.

There was no shortage of successors for leadership in the exploding witchcraft community.

"KING OF THE WITCHES"

Alex Sanders probably would have lived and died in obscurity had it not been for the rebirth of witchcraft as a religion. Born in 1926 in Manchester, England, Sanders spent much of his life drifting from one low-paying job to another and from one relationship to another. By the time he surfaced in witchcraft in the 1960s, he had a story of a family history in witchcraft and psychic powers. Sanders's own psychic powers seemed to be genuine, but whether he inherited them from family witches or learned them on his own is not certain.

Sanders joined in the witchcraft movement and established his coven. He was a natural showman and attracted attention and followers. By 1965 he claimed to have 1,623 initiates in 100 covens. His followers, he said, had named him "King of the Witches." The title had media appeal, and soon the press was calling Sanders the king of *all* witches. Many other witches, such as those who followed Gardner, were not happy with that.

Around the same time, Sanders met Maxine Morris, 20 years younger than him, and initiated her. They were married in 1967, and soon became famous for their "Alexandrian" brand of witchcraft, taught out of their home in the Notting Hill Gate area of London.

Their coven always worked in the nude, except for Sanders. "Witch law," he said, required him to be clothed. Like Gardner, the Sanderses initiated people who became leaders in the new Craft, among them Stewart and Janet Farrar, and Vivianne Crowley.

Sanders was knowledgeable about ceremonial magic, and added many elements of that to his brand of witchcraft.

Sanders's peak lasted until 1972, when he and Maxine separated. Both continued in the Craft on their own. In the 1980s Sanders developed lung cancer and died on April 30, 1988.

WITCHCRAFT GOES ABROAD

It did not take long for the new witchcraft to leave the shores of Britain. Initiates of the Gardnerian, Alexandrian, and other newly minted traditions were soon planting their seeds in Europe, North America, Australia, the Far East, and throughout the Pacific.

The most influential of the new witches in America was Raymond Buckland, a native of London with a Gypsy heritage. In 1962, Buckland and his wife, Rosemary, moved to the United States. Buckland had been drawn to the work of Gardner and Murray, and on a trip back to England in 1963, he was initiated into the Gardnerian tradition by Lady Olwen, one of Gardner's leading high priestesses. Buckland met Gardner that same year.

Rosemary took initiation, too, and the couple established a coven on Long Island, New York. The couple divorced, and Buckland continued his involvement in the craft, becoming one of the leading spokespersons and experts. He left the Gardnerian tradition and founded his own, Seax-Wica, a more open and democratic tradition.

A natural writer, Buckland began a prolific writing career in 1969, creating dozens of books, novels, screenplays, and divination tools.

The new witchcraft became part of a broader movement, a revival of interest in occultism, the supernatural, and mysticism. It caught on everywhere, especially on college campuses. Feminists liked the emphasis on the Goddess. Environmentalists liked the emphasis on honoring the sacred in nature. People who found their religions boring or too restricting liked the freedom promised by witchcraft. Witchcraft was "in."

FIFTY YEARS ON

Witchcraft as a religion is now more than 50 years old. Its first half-century was colorful, creative, and often chaotic. By the 1970s Murray's ideas of an unbroken, inherited religion were dead, and most Witches accepted the idea of the new Witchcraft as a reconstruction of old pagan ways.

There are dozens and dozens of traditions, blending existing religions, shamanism, ceremonial magic, folk magic, family lore, and old paganism. Witches write their own rituals. Most have abandoned Gardner's idea of practicing skyclad—working without clothes on isn't very practical. There are large churches, temples, and organizations, but no central authority or clergy. Witches value their independence.

Not everyone has appreciated the new religion, however. Conservative, mainstream critics still associate it with "devil worship" and evil. Witches have had to fight hard for civil rights, and for legal status as religious organizations—and for using a capital W in Witch and Witchcraft to distinguish themselves from "witchcraft" as an art of sorcery. The difference is often lost on outsiders.

Witchcraft—also called Wicca—is considered part of Neo-Paganism, other religious paths that have reconstructed old pagan ways. These new religions are among the fastest growing, attracting more and more new followers from every walk of life. As the movement continues to mature, Witches are addressing their social needs and concerns, and their interests in building lasting communities, lifestyles, and institutions. Second and third generation Witches are growing up.

Wicca and the Goddess

On a warm night, a group of witches gather on a hill. The sky and the landscape are lit with the sparkling radiance of the full moon. Their black robes blend into the darkness. They are alone.

They perform a ritual to cast and open a magic circle, and then they take their places around it. In the center is the coven's high priestess. Tonight, the night of the full moon, is the Goddess's night, and they are here to pay her honor by "drawing down the moon."

As a group, the coven raises energy by chanting and moving around the circle. The high priestess absorbs it, and she shifts into a light trance. When the energy feels right and she feels connected to a stream of divine light, she and the **high priest** deliver the most powerful and poetic rite of Wicca: the Charge of the Goddess.

If the energy is high and her powers strong, the high priestess is truly transformed and becomes a living embodiment of the Goddess. For the coven members standing in witness, the moment is magical, sacred, and holy. They are suspended in a timelessness that seems to touch the very center of creation.

The Charge of the Goddess is one of the most performed and important rituals in Wicca. The beauty and intent of it, to honor the Goddess and her presence in the world, stands in dramatic contrast to the demonic rituals described by witch hunters only a few centuries ago.

How did witchcraft make a 180-degree turn, from the dark and demonic to the sacred?

Figure 7.1 *Wiccans perform a ritual to open a magic circle, with a pentagram in the foreground.* (Fortean Picture Library)

Witchcraft "came out of the broom closet" in England with the repeal of an anti-witchcraft law in 1951. Did Gerald B. Gardner, who popularized witchcraft at this time, intend to establish a new religion? Or was he interested only in publicity, and so made up a romantic history?

Gardner claimed that witchcraft was "the Old Religion," a form of paganism unbroken and secret from ancient times. He said he had fragments of ancient rituals to prove it. The claims were dubious, and the fragments were uninspired. Luckily for Gardner, he met a woman who helped his credibility.

ENTER DOREEN VALIENTE

If Gerald Gardner can be called the "father" of modern Witchcraft, then the title of "mother" goes to Doreen Valiente. A native of south

London, Valiente was already well steeped in folk magic, ceremonial magic, and occultism by the time she heard about Gardner's New Forest coven. She had been casting her own folk magic spells since her teen years.

In 1952 Valiente read a newspaper article about a man named Cecil Williamson, who had opened the Folklore Centre of Superstition and Witchcraft on the Isle of Man. The article also mentioned the existence of a coven of witches in the New Forest area, near where Valiente and her husband lived.

Intrigued, Valiente wrote to Williamson to ask for more information. He passed the letter to Gardner, who answered it. Not long after that, they met over tea at the home of "Dafo," the woman Gardner said initiated him into the New Forest coven.

Gardner gave Valiente a copy of his novel, *High Magic's Aid*, to test her interest. She passed the test. In 1953 he initiated her as his first high priestess in a ritual conducted at Dafo's home. She took a **Craft name** of Ameth.

Valiente was knowledgeable about the occult and was a gifted writer and poet. She looked at Gardner's collection of rituals and fragments that made up his book of shadows and knew instinctively how to rework them. She saw a potential to witchcraft that Gardner missed.[1]

From 1954 to 1957 Valiente worked with Gardner to rewrite the rituals and create a foundation for witchcraft as a religion. At the time both were influenced by the ideas of Margaret Murray, that witchcraft was an old pagan religion. If it was, Valiente reasoned, then it surely needed to emphasize the Goddess more.

One of her most important contributions was her Charge of the Goddess, usually done in the Drawing Down the Moon ritual. Drawing Down the Moon was taken from ancient Greek beliefs that the witches of Thessaly possessed the power to command the moon to come down from the sky. By drawing down the moon, Wiccans connect with the Goddess, who is represented by the moon.

Gardner wrote the first version of the Charge, borrowing from Aleister Crowley and *Aradia*, a Tuscan witch legend recorded by

Charles Godfrey Leland. Valiente came up with her own version, which in turn has been modified by other witches. The following comes from Stewart and Janet Farrar, witches initiated by Alex Sanders:

The High Priest says:
  "Listen to the words of the Great Mother; she who was of old also called among men Artemis, Astarte, Athene, Dione, Melusine, Aphrodite, Cerridwen, Dana, Arianrhod, Isis, Bride, and by many other names."

The High Priestess says:
  "Whenever ye have need of any thing, once in the month, and better it be when the moon is full, then shall ye assemble in some secret place, and adore the spirit of me, who am Queen of all witches. There shall ye assemble, ye who are fain to learn all sorcery, yet have not won its deepest secrets; to these will I teach things that are yet unknown. And ye shall be free from slavery; and as a sign that ye be really free, ye shall be naked in your rites; and ye shall dance, sing, feast, make music and love, all in my praise. For mine is the ecstasy of the spirit, and mine also is joy on earth; for my law is love unto all beings. Keep pure your highest ideal; strive ever towards it; let naught stop you or turn you aside. For mine is the secret door which opens upon the Land of Youth, and mine is the cup of wine of life, and the Cauldron of Cerridwen, which is the Holy Grail of immortality. I am the gracious Goddess, who gives the gift of joy unto the heart of man. Upon earth, I give the knowledge of the spirit eternal; and beyond death, I give peace, and freedom, and reunion with those who have gone before. Nor do I demand sacrifice; for behold, I am the Mother of all living, and my love is poured out upon the earth."

The High Priest says:

 "Hear ye the word of the Star Goddess, she in the dust of whose feet are the hosts of heaven, whose body encircles the universe."

The High Priestess says:

 "I who am the beauty of the green earth, and the white Moon among the stars, and the mystery of the waters, and the desire of the heart of man, call unto thy soul. Arise, and come unto me. For I am the soul of nature, who gives life to the universe. From me all things proceed, and unto me all things must return; and before my face, beloved of Gods and of men, let thine innermost divine self be enfolded in the rapture of the infinite. Let my worship be within the heart that rejoiceth; for behold, all acts of love and pleasure are my rituals. And therefore let there be beauty and strength, power and compassion, honor and humility, mirth and reverence within you. And thou who thinkest to seek me, know thy seeking and yearning shall avail thee not unless thou knowest the mystery; that if that which thou seekest thou findest not within thee, thou wilt never find it without thee. For behold, I have been with thee from the beginning; and I am that which is attained at the end of desire."[2]

Valiente's towering contributions to witchcraft helped the movement get off the ground as a true religion. During the 1960s others added their own creativity and scholarship. It wasn't long before the new Witchcraft, or Wicca, was entirely different than the witchcraft of the Inquisition.

CENTRAL CONCEPTS

Wicca has many traditions, which have their own unique rituals and characteristics. There are core beliefs and practices that are shared among them:

Goddess and God

Wicca is a religion of polarity, or opposites, and a balance of masculine and feminine. The Goddess, also called the Lady, represents the feminine. The Horned God of nature (who is not the same as the Devil), also called the Lord, represents the masculine. The many gods and goddesses of pagan religions represent different aspects of Goddess and Horned God.

The Wiccan Rede

This is a creed that describes the basic philosophy of Wicca:

> Eight words the Wiccan Rede fulfill;
> An' it harm none, do what ye will.

The exact origin of the Wiccan Rede is uncertain. Gardner tried to pass it off as ancient, but he probably borrowed it from Aleister Crowley's magical Law of Thelema: "Do what thou wilt shall be the whole of the Law." It does not mean doing what you please, but refers to finding your true will, which will put you in harmony with everything in creation.

Gardner may have come up with The Wiccan Rede in order to help make modern Witchcraft more acceptable to the public.

Thirteen Principles of Wiccan Belief

The Council of American Witches formed in 1973–74 to define the principles of Wicca. Carl Weschcke, a Wiccan priest and president of Llewellyn Publications in St. Paul, Minnesota, led the council of 73 witches. Here is a summary of the principles:

1 Wiccan rituals are designed to attune participants to rhythms of nature, especially the phases of the Moon and the changes of the seasons.

2 Witches seek to live in a responsible balance and harmony with nature.

3   Power sometimes called "supernatural" is available to everyone.

4   Witches honor both the masculine and feminine sides of the Creative
Power in the universe.

5   The inner, spiritual world has as much importance as the outer,
physical world, and balancing both is important to a person's spiritual growth.

6   There is no central authority in Witchcraft. Leadership is based on
experience, knowledge, and wisdom.

7   Religion, magick, and wisdom in living combine to form a philosophy called *Witchcraft—the Wiccan Way*.

8   A person does not become a Witch by calling himself or herself one,
or by heredity, or collecting titles, degrees, and initiations. A Witch
seeks to master the inner self in order to live wisely and well, without
harm to others and in harmony with nature.

9   Life is a continuing evolution of spiritual development that gives
meaning to the Universe and a person's role in it.

10 Witches disagree that any religion or life philosophy is the "only
way," and they oppose any attempts to suppress religious freedom.

11 American Witches are not threatened by debates on the history,
origins, and validity of the Craft and its traditions and terminology.
They are concerned with the present and future.

12 Witches do not accept the concept of absolute evil, and do not worship "Satan" or "the Devil." Witches do not seek power by making
other people suffer.

13 Witches find health and well-being through Nature.

Threefold Law of Return, or Karma

This is more of an ethic than a law, and is also of uncertain origin. It
was first mentioned in print by Raymond Buckland in his book *Witchcraft: Ancient and Modern* in 1970.[3] It means that whatever one does
comes back magnified three times. It holds a warning that bad acts and

black magic will boomerang back in a more severe way—and also that good acts and magic will come back with multiplied blessings.

Reincarnation

Most Wiccans believe in reincarnation. After death, the soul goes to the **Summerland**, a Spiritualist term for heaven or the afterlife, where the soul prepares for rebirth.

Magic

Magic (sometimes spelled "magick" to distinguish it from stage magic tricks) is to be used for good, never for harm. Not all covens and traditions emphasize magic. Some use magic for ceremony, and others practice "practical magic," such as healing and the casting of spells.

Becoming a Witch/Wiccan

Sarah's night of initiation has finally arrived. Drawn to Wicca for several years, she has studied, read, and attended public Pagan gatherings. She has met Wiccans and finally found a coven of Witches whose ideals and personalities suit her own. They have invited her to join.

The initiation ceremony takes place on the night of a full moon, within a magic circle cast for the coven. Sarah will be initiated as a first-degree witch by the coven's high priest. She has prepared by taking a ritual bath of purification and by fasting.

In her initiation, she pledges to serve the Lady and Lord and dedicate herself to the principles of the Craft. She takes an oath of secrecy. The high priest anoints her and calls the blessings of the Lady and Lord upon her. She takes a Craft name, a secret magical name.

An initiation is like a rebirth, and tonight Sarah is reborn a Witch or Wiccan. She will train and work with her new spiritual family to forge a new way of life.

All spiritual traditions and religions have a point of entry: baptism, conversion, confirmation, initiation. They are ceremonies and rituals that symbolize a spiritual rebirth. In the early days of Wicca, most members followed standard rituals. A person could not be a witch unless he or she was initiated into an "official" coven. The right, or charter, to operate a coven had to be handed down through a lineage of initiations or family tradition.

Men were initiated by the high priestess, and women were initiated by the high priest. There were three levels in a coven: first degree, second degree, and third degree. All witches were called priestesses and priests. A minimum of one year and a day had to be spent at each level before a witch could be initiated into the next level. Once third degree was reached, a witch qualified to be a high priestess or high priest. These were the only persons who could officially "hive off" and start a new coven.

Today, there are almost as many variations of initiation rituals as there are traditions. Some feature ceremonial magic, while others have shamanic rituals that emphasize entering a trance. Some traditions that emphasize certain pantheons, or groups, of gods and goddesses—such as Egyptian or Norse—have even different initiation rituals. A tradition that emphasizes Native American spirituality may have a vision quest as part of its initiation. Some covens do not follow a three-level hierarchy. At the core of all traditions, however, is a pledge to Wicca.

Self-initiation has become increasingly popular, too. Many people want to become Wiccans but do not want to join a group. People design their own initiations, or follow guidelines given in books, and make a pledge or dedication to the Craft.

RESPONSIBILITIES

Regardless of how a person enters the Craft, they take on certain responsibilities besides their pledge. Ongoing training is very important in Wicca. New Witches are expected to study and learn about their chosen tradition, the Craft, mythology, esoteric lore, folklore, and magical lore. They must become skilled in conducting rituals and practicing magic, and demonstrate their skill to their fellow Wiccans.

In the old days, the teachings were kept secret, and initiates started their learning once they joined a coven. Those conditions have changed dramatically. A great deal of information is available through books and the Internet. Many initiates in the Craft have already learned quite a bit of material, and may even have become skilled in ritual and magic before they join a coven.

Some Wiccans have grown up in the Craft and have learned it from friends at an early age. Initiation is still important, however, to mark the new life as a Witch.

Wiccans also have a responsibility to attend coven meetings as much as possible. Wicca is oriented around small groups, and a coven becomes a close-knit magical unit.

COVENS, CHURCHES, AND TEMPLES

Wicca is the largest path of Paganism, also called Neo-Paganism. Wiccans are considered Pagans, but not all Pagans are Wiccans. Pagans have a wide variety of paths and traditions, too, which focus on the spiritual in the natural world.[1]

A coven may be small and independent, or it may belong to a larger organization or network, including ones that also have Pagan members. Some of the larger organizations are churches, schools, and public resource services; these usually have obtained legal status as nonprofit or religious organizations.

There is no exact number of members required for covens. According to "tradition" as established by Gardner, covens have 13 members. Some are smaller, and some larger. Generally, covens do not grow into dozens of members. They prefer to remain small and close-knit.

Covens are headed by a high priestess and a high priest. Below them are the **summoner** or **temple summoner**, a priest, and the **maiden** (a priestess), who assist them.

CRAFT NAME

It is customary for Wiccans to adopt a secret Craft name upon initiation. A new name may be taken upon each level of initiation if the

Witch advances up a hierarchy. The Craft name is the name by which the gods and goddesses know a Wiccan, as well as others in a coven.

BOOK OF SHADOWS

Upon initiation, a new Wiccan is given the coven's book of shadows, its collection of history, lore, rituals, and other Craft information. The term "book of shadows" seems to have originated with Gerald B. Gardner, but the tradition is based on real history. Handbooks of magical and folk healing and herbal lore have been passed down through families for generations.

In the old days each coven kept one handwritten copy of its book of shadows. It was lent to an initiate, who had to copy it by hand. She or he then added material to the personal copy as experience and

Figure 8.1 *A book of shadows like those presented to new Wiccans upon initiation into a coven.* (Fortean Picture Library)

training advanced. Books of shadow were supposed to be strictly secret, but in the 1970s, witches began publishing public versions of them.

Today, an initiate is likely to receive the traditional book of shadows in digital form, and keep it as a file in a computer.

Whether or not witches had secret books during the days of the Inquisition is a matter of debate. Few of the common people during that time could read or write. Most magical lore was passed orally from teacher to student. The only book mentioned by the witch hunters was the "Devil's book," supposedly a record of pacts made with the Devil.

Gardner may have based his tradition of the book of shadows upon magical handbooks called **grimoires**. The grimoires are collections of rituals, spells, and names of spirits. Most were written in the 1500s to 1700s, but they claimed ancient origins.

THE PENTACLE

The religious symbol of Wicca is the **pentacle**, an upright five-pointed star enclosed in a circle. The pentacle is an old and powerful symbol in magic. It has many symbolic meanings. For example, it represents the human being, with the points marking the head, hands, and feet. It also represents the four elements of air, earth, water, and fire, with the fifth element of spirit.

Pentacles are traced in the air in rituals, such as to evoke (summon) or banish (dismiss) spirits. A pentacle position can be taken as a posture, with feet spread apart and arms held straight out.

Many Wiccans like to wear pentacle pendants, rings, and bracelets. Pentacles are inscribed on books of shadow, on ritual robes and clothing, and etched into magical tools.

In 2007 American Wiccans finally earned the right to have the pentacle displayed on the gravestones of Wiccan military personnel. Wiccan and Pagan groups lobbied the U.S. Congress for this right for several years.

Figure 8.2 *A medallion shaped as a pentacle, the symbol of Wicca.* (Rebecca McEntee/Corbis Sygma)

Civil Liberties for Witches and Pagans

All religions have holy days, many of which become recognized as national holidays. Wiccans and Pagans have their holy days, too, but not everyone thinks they should be able to take time off to observe them.

Since Wicca and Paganism "came out" as organized religions in the mid-twentieth century, their followers have had to lobby, fight, and petition for their religious holidays. Their holy days are the eight changes of season known as the Wheel of the Year. They include the beginnings of the four seasons, and four equinox days, or half-way points in each season.

Government organizations have been slow to recognize Wicca and Paganism as religions, especially for civil servant employees.

In America, the American Civil Liberties Union (ACLU) has worked for recognition of Wiccan and Pagan holidays. Wiccans and Pagans also have established civil rights groups. In 1986 Laurie Cabot, the "Official Witch of Salem," was the key founder of the Witches' League for Public Awareness. The WLPA is an international organization that works against prejudices, discrimination, and misunderstandings about modern witches. The WLPA coordinates some of its efforts with law enforcement and organizations such as the ACLU.

Another organization involved in civil rights defenses is Circle Sanctuary, located in Wisconsin. Circle Sanctuary was incorporated as a nonprofit religious organization in Wisconsin in 1978. It helped to defend Wiccans and Pagans suffering from discrimination and harassment. In the mid-1980s U.S. Senator Jesse Helms and others introduced bills to Congress to prevent Wiccans and Pagans from obtaining nonprofit and tax-free—status as churches and religious organizations. Circle was among the lobbyists fighting against these measures, which failed to pass.

(continues)

(continued)

Some individual Wiccans and Pagans have filed lawsuits to secure their religious holidays. In 1986 Charles Arnold, an American Wiccan who moved to Canada, launched a legal case to have Wicca decriminalized by the Canadian government. It was a long and stressful process. Finally arbitrators ruled that Wicca did meet legal requirements for a religion. Arnold, who at the time worked at a college in Toronto, was granted a few paid Wiccan holidays.

Today, followers of Wicca and Paganism still run into hostility and opposition from people who dislike their practices, and who accuse them of devil worship. Every new religion has faced such difficulties. In the early days of Christianity, for example, followers were persecuted and even killed for their beliefs.

COVEN MEETINGS

Meetings called **"esbats"** are usually held at the full moon, and sometimes at the new moon. Many esbats are devoted to healing magic. Esbats traditionally end with cakes-and-ale, a communion of cake and natural beverages. After magical work and worship are officially closed, coven members usually relax with refreshments.

In addition to the esbats, coven members participate in seasonal festivals sometimes called "sabbats," described in Chapter 10. And, many participate in Pagan Pride days, public parades, and celebrations.

PRIVATE VERSUS PUBLIC

Many Wiccans like to follow their spiritual and magical practices in privacy. Others are interested in being active in a community. Many

Hedge Witches Keep Old Traditions Alive

Before the day of science and modern medicine, people relied upon folk remedies and magic for help with health and daily life. Every town and village had people, both women and men, who were skilled in providing such help. They were called by different names: witch, wizard, wise woman, wise man, **cunning man, cunning woman**, hex doctor, sorcerer. Even midwives—women who helped in the birthing of babies—were often persons who had magical skills. A modern term is "hedge witches," coined by an English solitary witch, Rae Beth. Hedge witch describes the way rural witches lived in their hedge-filled countryside.

These specialists usually were born with natural psychic ability. Their skill in seeing the future and knowing the thoughts of others gave them magical status. Sometimes the professions were passed down within families, inherited by one generation after another. Others found teachers and became apprentices. They knew herbal lore, and made medicines and magical potions. They cast spells for good and for harm.

Just as someone would visit a doctor today, people in the past consulted their local witches and wizards if they or their farm animals were sick. They paid for spells for blessings to provide prosperity, happiness, love, luck, and fertility. They received spells for protection against harm, especially spells that might be cast by their enemies.

Witches and other magical specialists who practiced in rural areas did not belong to covens or organizations. They were "solitaries," that is, they practiced alone. Some modern witches also prefer to practice alone. They may not consider themselves members of a Wiccan religion, but rather as specialists who keep old traditions alive. Like their predecessors in centuries past, they know herbal lore, and they cast

(continues)

(continued)

magical spells based on folk knowledge passed down orally through generations. They honor the old pagan deities.

Today, a person does not need to live in the remote countryside to be a hedge witch. Hedge witches can live in cities and suburban areas. Their name describes their approach to witchcraft and old traditions rather than the place they live.

Modern hedge witches have included some elements of modern Wicca in their practices. In earlier times, witches—like most people who lived in rural areas—were probably illiterate. They observed seasonal rites that were tied to agriculture cycles. Their spells included both Pagan and Christian elements and terms.

Wiccans feel it is important to make contributions of time and knowledge to building their spiritual community or family. Some covens belong to larger organizations that provide public education resources and social services.

Spellcraft

The setting is the basement of a private home, anywhere, in modern times. A Witch sits inside a magical circle that has been ritually cast with a small knife called an **athame** and marked with a white cord. She is working a spell to attract the right partner into her life.

The spell is cast with knots, a simple but effective form of magic, with a long tradition in folklore. In accordance with the beliefs of her Wiccan path, the Witch is not trying to influence a particular person, for that is considered the wrong use of magic. Rather, she is using magic to attract the unknown person who is meant to be with her.

She has composed a spell in the form of a charm, a little rhyming prayer:

> *The flower of love*
> *Blooms day and night*
> *Everything in life*
> *Goes right*

> *I have all the love*
> *That I desire*
> *Love lift me up*
> *Higher and higher*

While she recites the charm, she envisions the help of the Goddess in answering her request. She then ties knots in a nine-foot-long pink cord. The pink symbolizes love. The knots, according to magical lore, hold the power of the spell. She ties nine knots, reciting an old folk magic charm:

> *By the knot of one the spell's begun*
> *By the knot of two the spell is true*
> *By the knot of three so mote it be*
> *By the knot of four the open door*
> *By the knot of five the spell's alive*
> *By the knot of six the spell I fix*
> *By the knot of seven the gates of heaven*
> *By the knot of eight the hand of fate*
> *By the knot of nine the spell is mine!*[1]

Over the next nine days, she will untie one knot a week while focusing intense concentration on the spell. Untying the knot releases the energy of the spell.[2] In this way, she will release magical forces that will help bring about her goal: meeting the person who is meant to be her partner in life.

Witches cast spells in many ways. Some spells are done in rituals that involve a variety of special tools. Witches of old, who practiced folk magic, often had no formal tools and used whatever was handy in their kitchens and pantries.

TOOLS

The athame is a double-bladed knife that a Wiccan keeps for magical work. It is one of a variety of tools that symbolize the four elements, and the principles of the divine masculine and divine feminine. A cup or chalice symbolizes water, and also the Goddess. The athame, as well as the sword, symbolizes the element of fire or air, depending on tradition, and also the Horned God. Wands symbolize air, and pentacles—a disk inscribed with the five-pointed star—symbolize

Figure 9.1 *A Wiccan holds an athame during a ritual.* (Kirk Condyles/The Image Works)

earth. Many rituals involve having the symbols of the four elements present.

Many Wiccans keep cauldrons as tools, for mixing herbal recipes, and to symbolize water and the Goddess. Cauldrons filled with water can be used for scrying, a way of divining the future by gazing into a reflective surface. Cord magic—tying knots in colored cords as described above—is popular for spell-casting, and many Wiccans keep an assortment of cords on hand. They select colors to suit the purpose of a spell. For example, a green cord can be used for healing, abundance, and prosperity. Orange might be used for self-confidence. Even black can serve a purpose, such as for the elimination of something undesired.

Other tools can include crystals, images of gods and goddesses, mirrors, feathers, shells, and more. Wiccans acquire tools that "feel" right to them, and are creative in finding ritual uses for things.

If they have the space at home, Wiccans set up a small altar, where they keep their tools and images of gods and goddesses.

CLOTHING

Gerald B. Gardner insisted that witches worked with no clothes on, and for years many new Witches felt that they had to do the same in order to be authentic. There is no historical evidence for this practice as a part of witchcraft.[3] Gardner probably made it up because that is what he liked himself. Some Wiccans feel liberated by working "skyclad," as Gardner called it, while others prefer the comfort of clothing.

Many have robes and gowns specifically for magical work, decorated with symbols and magical words.

MAGIC CIRCLES

A magic circle is an enclosed sacred space for worship and magical work. It creates a controlled doorway to the spiritual world. It is protected space.

Figure 9.2 *Wiccans often keep cauldrons as tools, using them to mix herbal recipes and conduct rituals.* (Rebecca McEntee/Corbis Sygma)

Before a magic circle is cast, the energy in the working area is cleansed. A priest or priestess might do this symbolically by sweeping the air with a broom or by burning incense or sage. This removes negative energy.

A magic circle is cast by ritual. The circle may be drawn on a floor or the ground, or traced invisibly with an athame or wand. The movement to cast and open goes clockwise, called ***deosil***, from an Irish term *deiseal*, which means "a turning to the right." The movement to close a circle goes counterclockwise, or ***widdershins***, from an Anglo-Saxon term *with sith*, which means "to walk against."

Most magic circles are 9 feet in diameter, though they can vary in size. The points of the circle that mark the directions of east, south, west, and north, each have a significance, and a spiritual guardian that is summoned. The Goddess and Horned God are invoked. Depending on the tradition of the Craft, faeries, nature spirits, and guardians of the land may be invoked as well.

Once a circle is cast and the participants enter, they must not leave until the circle is closed. Closing a circle properly is important, for the doorway to the spiritual must be shut. Otherwise, according to the principles of magic, unwanted presences might be able to cross the barrier and enter the physical world.

The central work of the coven takes place within the magic circle. The gods are worshiped and honored there. Spell-casting, divination, channeling, trance, and healing work are done.

Initiates learn how to do **evocations** and **invocations** to summon spiritual presences. An evocation summons or requests a presence to manifest and witness or participate in the initiate's activities. In an invocation, the priest or priestess summons the spiritual energy for assistance. For example, a priestess invokes the Goddess in order to become a channel allowing the Goddess to speak.

SPELLS

A spell is an act of magic that is intended to accomplish a specific purpose. Spell-casting involves raising energy and calling upon higher forces and powers to help. Spells are ancient—human beings have always believed that supernatural powers can be summoned for help to achieve goals.

Spells can be either positive or negative. Good spells are sometimes called blessings, and negative spells are called curses and hexes.

Throughout history, spells have been cast for manipulating people and events to suit someone's purpose. Most Wiccans believe that is a wrong use of magic. Spells should be positive and never to harm or interfere in another person's life. Wiccan spell work ideally is a lot like praying for the highest good rather than for something specific. If negative spell work is undertaken, it is usually directed at stopping a

To Curse or Not to Curse

In magic, a curse is a spell that is intended to bring harm, destruction, or even death. Human beings have engaged in cursing throughout history. Cursing is a common form of revenge, like an "eye for an eye." **Ill-wishing** is another form of cursing, in which someone hopes that bad things will happen to another person.

In the lore of witchcraft, witches were believed to curse simply to be mean. People believed that anything bad that happened was probably a witch's curse. Today people know that many factors cause bad things to happen. But cursing is still a real magical power.

Most modern Witches and Wiccans say that cursing is immoral and should never be done. They say that magic should only be used for good. Some Wiccans say that cursing is okay under certain circumstances. For example, criminals such as convicted murderers, rapists, and molesters can be cursed. Cursing also is acceptable if a person is under any kind of attack by someone.

Others, however, say that even under extreme circumstances, cursing should not be done. The universal law of "cause and effect" will bring the curse back on the curser. This belief holds that whatever one does will come back to him or her, somehow, sometime, somewhere.

A compromise magical spell is called a "binding." A binding spell is intended to prevent someone from doing harm. It is used by many people of different religious traditions.

harmful behavior. For example, some Wiccans feel that spells to stop crimes and harmful behavior are justified.

Spell-casting can be done with written words, or spoken aloud, or even acted out. Herbs, colored candles, magical symbols, and magical tools are used. One old technique of spell-casting is to chant the purpose of the spell while tying a cord or long piece of fabric in knots. The knots symbolically hold the power of the spell. When the knots are untied, which might be done according to a timetable or phases of the moon, the power of the spell is released.

Another old technique of spell-casting involves poppets, which are dolls that symbolize a person or a desired outcome. The term "poppets" comes from a Middle English word *popet*, which means "small child" or "doll." Poppets can be actual dolls; in earlier times, doll-like figures were made of wax and clay. They are decorated according to a spell. For example, a poppet for healing might be decorated with a piece of clothing belonging to the sick person, or a lock of hair, or some nail clippings. A photograph can also be pinned to a poppet or a name can be written upon it.

The healing energy of the spell is directed into the poppet. According to the principle of sympathetic magic, the magical energy is transferred to the object of the spell, in this case, the sick person.

Spell-casting varies in importance in Wicca, with some covens and traditions emphasizing it more than others. Some people have a natural gift for spell-casting. For everyone, skill in spell-casting is built with practice and training within the coven.

RAISING ENERGY

Spell-casting requires the raising of psychic or spiritual energy. There are many ways for a group or individual to raise this energy, including chanting, drumming, dancing and other movements, knot tying, and singing. In magic, a person must raise as much emotional power as possible and direct all of it into the intent of the spell. The energy is released into the cosmos, like an arrow flying toward a target.

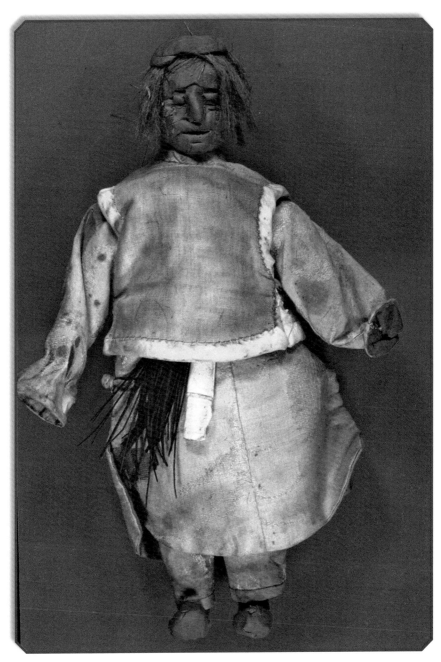

Figure 9.3 *Poppets, an old, spell-casting technique, often represent a person or a desired outcome.* (Fortean Picture Library)

One way to raise group energy is called the "cone of power." The witches dance or chant, moving around the magic circle and increasing their speed. They hold an image or thought of their purpose. They visualize energy in the shape of a cone over the group. When the high priestess or high priest senses that the energy is at its peak, the group sends the energy out through the tip of the cone.

FAMILIARS

Many Wiccans have familiars, but they are not the demonic animals and insects described by the witch hunters of the Inquisition. Animals are valued for their psychic sensitivity and companionship, and many of them are invited to participate in magical work. When pets die, some Wiccans believe they reincarnate and come back as other animals in order to continue their personal relationships and magical partnerships.

Wiccan Celebrations

*E*very religion has its holy days, and Wicca is no exception. Wiccan holidays are not oriented around the birthdays of people or the anniversaries of events in history. They coincide with the natural cycle of seasons.

Before the era of big cities, industry, and technology, human life was ruled by the cycles of nature. As the seasons changed, so did daily life and activities concerning crops and farm animals. Over the course of history, people created festivals to mark the changes of seasons, to give thanks for the old and to welcome the new, and to honor the gods and goddesses and ask for their blessings. Every season had its own deities who governed it.

Technology makes people less dependent on seasonal changes, but they are still controlled by Mother Earth. When she sleeps in winter, life becomes quieter, and when she awakens in spring and blooms in summer, people are active and energetic.

The Wheel of the Year is the Wiccan and Pagan calendar of holy days that celebrate the eternal turning of the cycles of nature. Wiccans and Pagans look back into the past to see how people marked and celebrated seasonal changes. Modern rituals are reconstructions of old ones. In some cases, there is no historical evidence for certain rites, so new ones have been created. There are no central, unified rites.

The Wheel of the Year has eight holy days or seasonal festivals. The festivals are also called sabbats, although the use of that term has declined due to its associations with the demonic sabbats of the Inquisition.

The major festivals occur at the change-of-season points: the summer and winter solstices, and the spring and autumn equinoxes. There are four "in-between" festivals that mark certain times in old agrarian calendars. The seasonal holidays are fire festivals, especially the solstices. They are derived from bonfire rituals that were performed to help the sun keep its course in the sky at these changes of season. The equinoxes were not "official" old pagan holidays, but have been added to the wheel in modern times.

As Christianity absorbed pagan practices, it substituted its holidays for pagan ones. For example, All Saint's Day replaced Samhain, and popular Halloween celebration customs also were substituted.

Celebrations involve gatherings, small groups, and individual observances. There are bonfires, rituals and religious services, dancing, music, and special foods, just like the holidays of other religions. Sometimes a festival may span several days. Since Wicca is a creative religion, the structures and specific rituals of the festivals can vary. The common intent is to honor the divine in nature, especially as personified by the gods and goddesses. Celebrating the Wheel of the Year is an important part of Wicca.[1]

Here are descriptions of the seasonal festivals, including traditional meanings and observances, and modern observances. Many customs followed today have ancient roots. Since the exact starts of the solstices and equinoxes change, the dates for those festivals are "on or about."

DECEMBER 21: YULE

Yule, or the Winter Solstice, sets the Wheel of the Year in motion. In the northern hemisphere, it is the shortest day of the year, mid-winter. "Yule" comes from the name of the Norse god Jul, meaning "wheel."

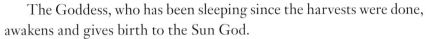

The Goddess, who has been sleeping since the harvests were done, awakens and gives birth to the Sun God.

The Yule log, candle lights, and tree lights symbolize the old fire festivals. Decorations of evergreen, holly, ivy, and mistletoe symbolize the renewed cycle of fertility.

FEBRUARY 1: IMBOLC/IMBOLG

Imbolc (pronounced iv'-olc) is a Celtic term for "in the belly." It represents the start of spring, the growing of the Sun God, and the stirring of nature.

In earlier times, Imbolc was a purification fire festival called the "Feast of Lights." For the Celts, Imbolc celebrated the great goddess Brigid, or Brigit, who rules fire, fertility, crops, livestock, poetry, wisdom, and household arts. Bonfires and processions of lights were hallmarks of this festival.

Imbolc is a time to clean out the old to make way for the new, to light candles to help the young Sun God, and to eat nuts and seeds.

MARCH 21: SPRING EQUINOX

The Spring Equinox marks the time when day and night are equal in length. Spring Equinox was not an official old pagan festival, though various festivals did take place around this time of year. Modern Pagans sometimes call it "Ostara."

The equinox symbolizes the Sun God gaining strength. Colored eggs are a symbol of fertility for this festival.

MAY 1: BELTANE

Like Samhain, Beltane (or May Day), was a major fire festival among Celtic pagans. It marks the start of summer when the natural world is rushing toward its peak. "Beltane" is derived from the Irish Gaelic word *Bealtaine*, or "Bel-fire." Bel is the Irish god of light. In earlier

Figure 10.1 *Two Wiccan high priests celebrate the Spring Equinox.* (Rebecca McEntee/Corbis Sygma)

times, Beltane was a great fertility festival, for it marked the union of the Goddess and God.

Beltane bonfires were believed to bring fertility and plenty to homes and the land. Rites were done for protection against illness and misfortune. There were dances around maypoles. It was a time for couples to form and relationships to start. Where faery lore was strong, offerings of food were left out for them.

Beltane is a time to wear and decorate with brightly colored flowers, ribbons, and garlands.

JUNE 21: MIDSUMMER

The Summer Solstice is the oldest and most widespread of European Pagan festivals. At the height of summer's glory, the longest day of the year, the Sun God dies. The natural world has reached its full glory and will begin its decline into autumn.

Midsummer is the time to harvest many herbs and plants for their magical and medicinal powers, and to make contact with faeries, who are out celebrating this time of year, too. Midsummer is a good time for blessings of luck, and for magic in general.

Figure 10.2 *This horn staff pays homage to the Horned God and serves as a symbol of authority. It may be used to invoke deities or direct ritual energy.* (Rebecca McEntee/Corbis Sygma)

AUGUST 1: LUGHNASADH

Lughnasadh, pronounced loo'-na-sah, means "to give in marriage." It symbolizes the marriage of heaven and earth. It is a time of harvests and of making marriage contracts. Marriage now forecasts birth at Beltane, nine months away.

In Irish lore, the festival celebrates the marriage between the god Lugh, the god of light and wisdom, and the goddess Eriu. Eriu is ugly, and her union with Lugh transforms her into a beauty. She personifies the land of Ireland itself.

Lughnasadh rites are of thanksgiving for the first harvests. The first corn is cut at this time.

Another name for this festival is Lammas (lahm'-mahs), which comes from an Old English term for "loaf" or "mass." Lammas was a fruit and grain festival, and a time when tenant farmers had to pay their rent with a portion of their harvests.

Lughnasadh/Lammas is a time to give thanks for everything one enjoys in life. Harvest breads are important in thanksgiving rites.

SEPTEMBER 21: AUTUMN EQUINOX

Once again, day and night are equal. Little evidence exists that the Celts officially celebrated the Autumn Equinox; the festival balances the modern Wheel of the Year. "Mabon," a Welsh proper name, was introduced in the 1970s to give the festival a Celtic sound.

The Autumn Equinox is the time of a second round of harvests and of the first preparations for winter.

For many, this is the Pagan Thanksgiving, a time to have feasts with family and friends, make wine, and plant bulbs for the spring.

OCTOBER 31: SAMHAIN

Samhain is a Celtic term for "end of summer," and is pronounced sow'-en, with the "sow" sounded as in "ow." Samhain heralds winter and the third and final harvests. Provisions are made for sustaining home and community through the winter.

In earlier times, a community bonfire would be built, and the fires in home hearths would be put out and relit from the community fire to symbolize this change. Things were stored and put away, and homes and farms were readied for the cold months to come.

Samhain is the time when the veil between the worlds is the thinnest. Spirits and the dead are able to come into the world very easily on Samhain night. In earlier times, it was believed that spirits would make trouble. Rituals to honor the dead would keep them happy. People made special offerings of food and dressed in disguises to fool spirits. The customs of Halloween trick-or-treating and divination games, especially to know the identity of a future spouse, evolved from Samhain traditions.

Samhain is a good time for divination, making contact with the spirit realms, and honoring the ancestral dead.

Timeline

1086   Start of the Crusades

1184   First papal bull ordering inquisitions of heretics

1227–33   Pope Gregory IX expands the Inquisition

1484   Pope Innocent VIII makes witchcraft a heresy

1488   The *Malleus Maleficarum* is published

1500s–1600s   Height of the Inquisition and witch hunts

1587–94   Treves, Germany, witch panics

1590–91   Trials of John Fian and North Berwick Witches, Scotland

1598   Loyse Maillat witch trials in Jura, France

1604   England enacts Witchcraft Law with severe punishments

1645–47   Matthew Hopkins reigns as "Witchfinder Generall" in England

1692   Salem witch trials begin

1693   Last witch executed in Salem witch trials

1700s   Inquisition comes to an end

1700s   German immigrants to America establish "powwowing"

1717   Richard Noyes dies, curse of executed witch blamed

1735   New Witchcraft Law in England reduces punishments for witchcraft

1802   John George Hohman publishes the *Long Lost Friend* of powwowing magic

1849   The *Sixth and Seventh Books of Moses* handbook of folk magic is published in Germany

1851   Nathaniel Hawthorne publishes *House of Seven Gables*, inspired by Salem witch trials

1929   John Blymire hex murder trial in Pennsylvania

1939   Gerald B. Gardner is initiated into the New Forest coven in England

1951   Britain repeals the 1735 Witchcraft Act, legalizing witchcraft

1954   Gardner publishes *Witchcraft Today*, the first major modern book about witches, by a witch

1960s   Gardnerian and Alexandrian traditions of Witchcraft spread around the world

1964   Gardner dies

1980   Circle Sanctuary receives federal recognition as a church from the United States government

1985   Charles Arnold launches legal case to have witchcraft decriminalized in Canada

1986   Laurie Cabot and others form the Witches' League for Public Awareness to fight prejudice and discrimination

1988   Alex Sanders dies

1993   Salem, Massachusetts, dedicates memorial to victims of 1692 witch trials

1998   Pope John Paul II apologizes for the Inquisition

2007   Wiccans win the right to have the pentacle, the symbol of their religion, displayed on headstones in veterans' cemeteries

Glossary

ATHAME   A small, double-bladed knife used in magic, ceremonial rituals, and spellcraft

BINDING   A spell to stop or prevent undesirable behavior or events; a modern replacement for curses

BLASTING   The ability of a witch to block or destroy the fertility of people, animals, and crops; during Inquisition times, it was a power attributed to witches, who were blamed for crop failures, livestock birthing problems, infertility, childbirth problems, and personal problems

CEREMONIAL MAGIC   Magic intended to exalt or raise human consciousness to contact with the gods, the divine, and higher spiritual powers

CHARM   A "little prayer," a magical incantation for spell-casting; can be written or spoken

COVEN   A small group of Witches or Wiccans who work together, and add members by invitation only

CRAFT   A term used for Wicca

CRAFT NAME   A Witch's secret magical name, taken upon initiation

CUNNING MAN OR WOMAN   A practitioner of folk magic

CURSE   A spell to harm or kill

DEOSIL   Clockwise movement to cast a magic circle

ESBAT   Term used by some modern Wiccans for monthly coven meetings at the full and new moons

EVIL EYE   The ability to cause misfortune and death by looking at someone

EVOCATION   A magical ritual to summon a spirit, entity, or deity, either as an external presence or as an internal force within a person.

FAMILIAR   A demon or spirit that takes on the form of an animal, bird, or insect and serves a witch.

GRIMOIRE   A handbook of magical instructions for conjuring spirits and casting spells

HEX   A Pennsylvania Dutch term for spell, either good or bad, though usually associated with bad; derived from the German word *hexe*, for "witch"

HIGH PRIEST   The male head of a coven, who represents the Horned God and the divine masculine

HIGH PRIESTESS   The female head of a coven, who represents the Goddess and the divine feminine

ILL-WISHING   A type of curse that involves intense thinking of bad thoughts about someone

IMP   A small demon, usually kept in a bottle or jar, who performs tasks on command

INVOCATION   A magical ritual to invite a spirit, deity or entity to make itself present, and to use its powers to grant requests.

MAGIC CIRCLE   A circular working space for magical work, cast, opened, and closed by ritual

MAIDEN   A Wiccan priestess who assists a coven's high priestess and high priest

NECROMANCY   Calling upon the dead for divination; in ancient times, the power of some witches to raise corpses temporarily to life in order to ask them questions

PENTACLE   Five-pointed star enclosed within a circle, the religious symbol of Wicca

POPPET   A doll, usually made out of wax, clay, or cloth, which substitutes for a real person in spell-casting. Spells projected onto a poppet are supposed to affect the victim in the same way.

POWWOWER   A Pennsylvania Dutch term for a person with power to heal, cast spells, and make or break curses

SABBAT   A festive meeting of witches; derived from sabbath or *shabbath*, the Hebrew term for "cease or rest"; in times of the witch hunts, referred to infernal gatherings with the devil and demons; In modern Wicca, refers to the holy days of seasonal change and celebration

SCRYING   Divining the future by gazing into a reflective surface, such as a mirror, bowl of water, piece of metal, or a crystal

SKYCLAD   Gerald B. Gardner's term for ritual nudity

SUMMERLAND   Wiccan term, borrowed from Spiritualism, for the afterlife

SUMMONER/TEMPLE SUMMONER   A Wiccan priest who assists the high priest and high priestess

TRADITION   A path within Wicca or Paganism, comparable to a denomination within Christianity; maybe founded by anyone

WIDDERSHINS   Counterclockwise movement to close a magic circle

Endnotes

CHAPTER 1

1. Georg Luck, "Witches and Sorcerers in Classical Literature," in *Witchcraft and Magic in Europe: Ancient Greece and Rome* (London: The Athlone Press, 1999), 120.

2. Ibid., 182.

3. Jeffrey B. Russell, *A History of Witchcraft* (London: Thames and Hudson, 1980), 12.

4. Paul Tice, Foreword in *Demonology* by King James I of England (San Diego: The Book Tree, 2002), 3.

CHAPTER 2

1. Keith Thomas, *Religion and the Decline of Magic* (New York: Charles Scribner's Sons, 1971), 525.

2. Anne Llewellyn Barstow, *Witchcraze: A New History of the European Witch Hunts* (San Francisco: Pandora/Harper Collins, 1994), 179-181.

CHAPTER 3

1. Paul Tice, *op. cit.*, 3.

2. Francesco-Maria Guazzo, *Compendium Maleficarum* (Secaucus, N.J.: University Books, 1974), 15.

3. Ibid., 15-16.

CHAPTER 4

1. David W. Kriebel, *Powwowing Among the Pennsylvania Dutch* (University Park, Pa.: Penn State University Press, 2007), 13-14.

2. Ibid., 22-23.

CHAPTER 5

1. Charles Upham, *History of Witchcraft and Salem Village* (Boston: Wiggin and Lunt, 1867), 314.

2. John Putnam Demos, *Entertaining Satan: Witchcraft and the Culture of Early New England* (New York: Oxford University Press, 2004), 59.

3. Ibid., 300-301.

CHAPTER 6

1. Margaret A. Murray, *The Witch-Cult in Western Europe* (London: Oxford University Press, 1921), 186-194.

2. Keith Thomas, *Religion and the Decline of Magic* (New York: Charles Scribner's Sons, 1971), 525.

3. Ronald Hutton, *The Triumph of the Moon: A History of Modern Pagan Witchcraft* (Oxford: Oxford University Press, 1999), 206-207.

CHAPTER 7

1. Doreen Valiente, *The Rebirth of Witchcraft* (London: Robert Hale, 1989), 65-66.

2. Janet and Stewart Farrar, *A Witches' Bible Compleat* (New York: Magickal Childe, 1984), 297-298.

3. Raymond Buckland, *Witchcraft: Ancient and Modern* (New York: House of Collectibles, 1970).

CHAPTER 8

1. Isaac Bonewits, *Bonewits's Essential Guide to Witchcraft and Wicca* (New York: Citadel Press Books, 2006), 105-106.

2. Raymond Buckland, *The Witch Book: The Encyclopedia of Witchcraft, Wicca, and Neo-paganism* (Detroit: Visible Ink Press, 2002), 470.

3. Shelley Rabinovitch and James Lewis, *The Encyclopedia of Modern Witchcraft and Neo-Paganism* (New York: Citadel Press, 2002), 289.

CHAPTER 9

1. Folk charm from the collection of the Museum of Witchcraft, Boscastle, Cornwall, England.

2. Raymond Buckland, *Buckland's Complete Book of Witchcraft* (St. Paul: Llewellyn Publications, 1986), 162.

3. Hutton, *op. cit.*, 231.

CHAPTER 10

1. Christopher Penczak, *The Inner Temple of Witchcraft: Magic Meditation and Psychic Development* (St. Paul: Llewellyn Publications, 2003), 46.

Further Resources

The following are the Web sites of some of the organizations devoted to networking, information, and public education, serving the Wiccan and Pagan communities:

Children of Artemis
http://www.witchcraft.org

Circle Sanctuary
http://www.circlesanctuary.org

Covenant of the Goddess
http://www.cog.org

Pagan Awareness Network
http://www.paganawareness.net.au

The Pagan Federation
http://www.paganfed.org

Witches' League for Public Awareness
http://www.celticcrow.com

Witchvox
http://www.witchvox.com

Bibliography

Ankarloo, Bengt and Stuart Clark, eds. *Ancient Greece and Rome.* Witchcraft and Magic in Europe, vol. 2, London: The Athlone Press, 1999.

Adler, Margot. *Drawing Down the Moon.* Revised ed. New York: Penguin, 2006.

Barstow, Anne Llewellyn. *Witchcraze: A New History of the European Witch Hunts.* San Francisco: Pandora/Harper Collins, 1994.

Beth, Rae. *Hedge Witch: A Guide to Solitary Witchcraft.* London: Robert Hale, 1990.

Bonewits, Isaac. *Bonewits's Essential Guide to Witchcraft and Wicca.* New York: Citadel Press Books, 2006.

Buckland, Raymond. *The Witch Book: The Encyclopedia of Witchcraft, Wicca, and Neopaganism.* Detroit: Visible Ink Press, 2002.

———. *Buckland's Complete Book of Witchcraft.* St. Paul: Llewellyn Publications, 1986.

Crowley, Vivianne. *Wicca: The Old Religion in the New Millennium.* Revised ed. London: Thorsons/Harper Collins, 1996.

Deacon, Richard. *Matthew Hopkins: Witch Finder General.* London: Frederick Muller, 1976.

Demos, John Putnam. *Entertaining Satan: Witchcraft and the Culture of Early New England*, 2d ed. New York: Oxford University Press, 2004.

Farrar, Janet and Stewart. *A Witches' Bible Compleat.* New York: Magickal Childe, 1984.

Farrar, Janet, and Gavin Bone. *Progressive Witchcraft: Spirituality, Mysteries & Training in Modern Wicca.* Franklin Lakes, N.J.: New Page Books, 2004.

Gardner, Gerald B. *Witchcraft Today.* London: Rider & Co., 1954.

Gardner, Gerald B. *The Meaning of Witchcraft.* New York: Magickal Childe, 1982.

Guazzo, Francesco-Maria. *Compendium Maleficarum.* Secaucus, N.J.: University Books, 1974.

Guiley, Rosemary Ellen. *The Encyclopedia of Witches, Witchcraft & Wicca*, 3d ed. New York: Facts On File, 2008.

Hutton, Ronald. *The Triumph of the Moon: A History of Modern Pagan Witchcraft.* Oxford: Oxford University Press, 1999.

Johns, June. *King of the Witches: The World of Alex Sanders.* New York: Coward-Mc-Cann, Inc., 1969.

Kriebel, David W. *Powwowing Among the Pennsylvania Dutch.* University Park, Pa.: Penn State University Press, 2007.

Lea, Henry Charles. *The History of the Inquisition in the Middle Ages.* New York: Macmillan, 1908.

Lipp, Deborah, and Isaac Bonewits. *The Study of Witchcraft: A Guidebook to Advanced Wicca.* York Beach, Me.: Weiser Books, 2007.

Murray, Margaret A. *The Witch-Cult in Western Europe.* London: Oxford University Press, 1921.

Penczak, Christopher. *The Inner Temple of Witchcraft: Magic Meditation and Psychic Development.* St. Paul: Llewellyn Publications, 2003.

Rabinovitch, Shelley and James Lewis. *The Encyclopedia of Modern Witchcraft and Neo-Paganism.* New York: Citadel Press, 2002.

Russell, Jeffrey B. *A History of Witchcraft.* London: Thames and Hudson, 1980.

Starhawk. *The Spiral Dance.* Rev. ed. San Francisco: HarperOne, 1999.

Upham, Charles. *History of Witchcraft and Salem Village.* Boston: Wiggin and Lunt, 1867.

Valiente, Doreen. *The Rebirth of Witchcraft.* London: Robert Hale, 1989.

Index

Page numbers in *italics* indicate images.

About the Author and Consulting Editor

ROSEMARY ELLEN GUILEY is one of the foremost authorities on the paranormal. Psychic experiences in childhood led to her lifelong study and research of paranormal mysteries. A journalist by training, she has worked full time in the paranormal since 1983, as an author, presenter, and investigator. She has written 31 nonfiction books on paranormal topics, translated into 13 languages, and hundreds of articles. She has experienced many of the phenomena she has researched. She has appeared on numerous television, documentary, and radio shows. She is also a member of the League of Paranormal Gentlemen for Spooked TV Productions, a columnist for *TAPS Paramagazine*, a consulting editor for *FATE* magazine, and writer for the "Paranormal Insider" blog. Ms. Guiley's books include *The Encyclopedia of Angels, The Encyclopedia of Magic and Alchemy, The Encyclopedia of Saints, The Encyclopedia of Vampires, Werewolves, and Other Monsters*, and *The Encyclopedia of Witches and Witchcraft*, all from Facts On File. She lives in Maryland and her Web site is http://www.visionaryliving.com.